PEN AND INK

PEN AND INK

PAPERS ON SUBJECTS OF MORE OR LESS IMPORTANCE

BY

BRANDER MATTHEWS

Essay Index Reprint Series

BOOKS FOR LIBRARIES PRESS
FREEPORT, NEW YORK

First Published 1888
Reprinted 1971

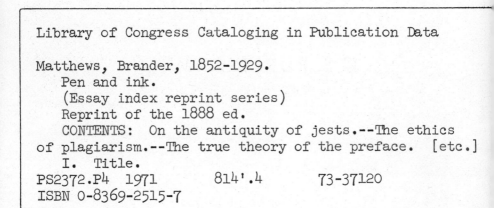

Library of Congress Cataloging in Publication Data

Matthews, Brander, 1852-1929.
    Pen and ink.
    (Essay index reprint series)
    Reprint of the 1888 ed.
    CONTENTS: On the antiquity of jests.--The ethics
of plagiarism.--The true theory of the preface. [etc.]
    I. Title.
PS2372.P4 1971   814'.4   73-37120
ISBN 0-8369-2515-7

PRINTED IN THE UNITED STATES OF AMERICA
BY
NEW WORLD BOOK MANUFACTURING CO., INC.
HALLANDALE, FLORIDA 33009

TO

E. L. BURLINGAME

IN GRATITUDE FOR COUNSEL

PREFACE

The author desires to declare here his belief that this is the most interesting, the most entertaining, and the most instructive book of the decade: — his reasons for making this bold assertion in this place will be found fully set forth on pp. 50–66.

B. M.

CONTENTS

"*Pen and Ink,*" *by A. Lang* . . . . *xiii*

I   *On the Antiquity of Jests* *1*

II   *The Ethics of Plagiarism* *22*

III   *The True Theory of the Preface* . . . *50*

IV   *The Philosophy of the Short-story* . . *67*

V   *Two Latter-day Lyrists* *95*

        I   *Frederick Locker*

        II   *Austin Dobson*

VI   *The Songs of the Civil War* *140*

VII   *On the French spoken by those who do not speak French* *168*

VIII   *Poker-talk* *187*

"*An Epistle to the Author,*" *by H. C. Bunner* *227*

PEN AND INK.

Ye wanderers that were my sires,
   Who read men's fortunes in the hand,
Who voyaged with your smithy fires
   From waste to waste across the land,
Why did you leave for garth and town
   Your life by heath and river's brink?
Why lay your Gipsy freedom down
   And doom your child to Pen and Ink?

You wearied of the wild-wood meal
   That crowned, or failed to crown, the day,
Too honest or too tame to steal,
   You broke into the beaten way:
Plied loom or awl like other men
   And learned to love the guinea's chink.
Oh, recreant sires, who doomed me then
   To earn so few—with Pen and Ink!

Where it hath fallen the tree must lie.
   'Tis over-late for ME to roam.
Yet the caged bird who hears the cry
   Of his wild fellows fleeting home

May feel no sharper pang than mine,
  Who seem to hear, whene'er I think,
Spate in the stream and wind in pine
  Call me to quit dull Pen and Ink.

For then the Spirit wandering,
  That sleeps within the blood, awakes;
For then the summer and the spring
  I fain would meet by streams and lakes.
But ah, my birthright long is sold,
  But custom chains me, link on link,
And I must get me, as of old,
  Back to my tools, to Pen and Ink.

A. LANG.

PEN AND INK

ON THE ANTIQUITY OF JESTS.

HERE are not a few very interesting and instructive books waiting to be written. Two goodly tomes there are, for example, which I am anxious to own,—the 'Anecdote History of Private Theatricals,' and 'A Historical Treatise on Scene-Painting and Stage-Mechanism.' Unfortunately nobody has yet thought it worth his while to write either of them, though it would be difficult to find anywhere two books about the stage more entertaining, more useful, and easier to put together. But a book which I would receive with more welcome and review more willingly even than these is the 'Authentic Jest-Book, chronologically arranged, with exact references to the original authorities and a collation of the parallel passages in other authors.' It may be thought that of jest-books we have a many, and that, at best, they are but dreary reading. And so it is. But the 'Authentic Jest-Book' is wholly unlike any other collection of jokes and gibes and repartees and witticisms; it is unlike them all, and better than any of them. In the ordinary gathering of merry jests, whether it be the collection of Hierocles, the Greek, or of Abou-na-wass, the Persian, whether it be the 'Moyen de Parvenir,' the compilation of some contemporary of Rabelais, or the 'Gesta Romanorum' growing together in monkish hands, whether it be the humorous anthology of the worthy Poggio or that credited to the unworthy Joseph Miller, in any and all of the recognized receptacles of the waifs and strays of wit and humor, there is one marked, permanent, and fatal defect : the most of the jokes are unidentified and unauthenticated ; they are set down as they were familiar in men's mouths at the time when Poggio and Hierocles and the double of Joseph Miller and their fellows went about taking notes. In other words, no effort has been made hitherto to show the genesis of jests, and to declare with precision and with authority just when a given joke was first made and just what transformations and adventures it has since undergone.

The jest-book I want is one giving chapter and verse for every laugh in it. In ' L'Esprit dans l'Histoire' and in 'L'Esprit des Autres,' Edouard Fournier made an attempt along the right path;

and he was followed aptly and promptly by
Mr. Hayward in the essay on the 'Pearls and
Mock-Pearls of History.' Fournier and Hayward
succeeded in showing that many an accepted witti-
cism is a very Proteus, reappearing again and again
with a change of face. Other jokes are, like Cagli-
ostro, turning up once in a century quite as
young as ever. There is, for instance, a story told
by Lord Stair, called the politest man in France
—because he obeyed the king's request and
jumped into the royal carriage before his majesty.
Lord Stair bore a singular resemblance to Louis
XIV., who was moved to ask him if Lord Stair's
mother had ever been to Paris ; to which Lord
Stair replied, "No, your majesty, but my father
has." The same story is told of Henri IV. and a
certain gentleman of Gascony. It can be found in
Macrobius, where it is related of a general who
came from Spain to the court of the Cæsars.
Now, in the 'Authentic Jest-Book,' this anecdote
would reappear in an English translation of the
exact words of Macrobius, with a note setting
forth the revival of the retort under Henri IV. and
Louis XIV. : no doubt it has been told of many
another monarch who was the father of his people
in the fashion of the *roi vert-galant*. Moore, as
in duty bound, sets down Sheridan's light-hearted

jest while he watched the burning of Drury Lane Theatre from the coffee-house where he was sipping a glass of sherry—" Surely a man may take a glass of wine at his own fireside!" This is a saying quite worthy of Sheridan, and one which he was quite capable of making ; but Moore, with a wise scepticism, suggested that it " may have been, for aught I know, like the Wandering Jew, a regular attendant upon all fires since the time of Hierocles."

There is, indeed, a metempsychosis of professional jokes. A merry jest about a preacher or a player or a physician is reincarnated in every generation. It is like royalty, it never dies—*Le roi est mort! Vive le roi!* Garrick's death eclipses the gayety of nations, but the stroke of humor which told for or against Garrick soon tells for or against Grimaldi. By a sort of apostolic succession, the anecdotes about a popular clergyman pass to the clergyman who succeeds him in popularity. Two of these perennial tales—one about a player, and the other about a preacher—have had an exceptionally strong hold on life. In the first a severe hypochondriac consults a physician, who advises recreation: " You should see Liston!" " I am Liston!" answers the severe hypochondriac. This is told of Grimaldi and of many another comic performer before and since his time. The earliest instance I have been able to find is in connection with Dominique, the famous arlequin of the Comédie-Italienne under Louis XIV. Arlequin Dominique was ready of speech, as an anecdote proves which has yet only one hero : the monarch was fond of the mimic, and seeing him thirsty one day, bade a servant give him a goblet filled to the brim. Now the goblet was of gold, so Arlequin slyly queried, "And the wine, too, your majesty?" But this is a digression.

The second story relates to a certain popular preacher, who on a sultry summer morning arose in his pulpit and wiped his forehead and said, "It is damned hot!" And when the congregation were properly shocked into wakefulness, he said, "Such were the words which met my ears this morning as I entered this house of worship!" and then he proceeded to preach a vigorous sermon against the sin of profanity. In the article which an important London weekly devoted to the celebration of Mr. Spurgeon's fifty years of ministry, this saying and this sermon were placed in the mouth of Mr. Spurgeon. In the United States Mr. Henry Ward Beecher was generally supposed to have said them—there are not wanting those who declare that they heard him—in spite of the eloquent protests and denial of his sister, Mrs. Harriet Beecher Stowe. But Rowland Hill preceded both Mr. Beecher and Mr. Spurgeon as the protagonist of this little sacred play ; and Robert Hall had appeared in the part before Rowland Hill. Who the real originator may be will not be known with certainty until the ' Authentic Jest-Book ' appears.

One class of anecdote should be excluded scrupulously from my model collection. It is the anecdote unvouched for by a recognizable proper name as one of the *dramatis personæ*. It is the anecdote which relates us the *faits et gestes* of " a certain Oxford scholar " or " a well-known wit " or " a foolish fellow." These anonymous tales are as unworthy of credence as an anonymous letter. A merry jest ought always to be accompanied by the name of the hero, necessarily for publication and as a guarantee of good faith. When the tale is tagged to a man whose name we know, investigation is possible and we may get at the truth. But these nameless stories are of no country and of no century—rather are they of all nations and of all times. It has been well said that Irish bulls were calves in Greece. There is a familiar Irish anecdote, not to be told here, though innocent enough, which turns on the continuance of the pattering of the rain-drops. This was confided to me a few years ago in America as the latest importation from the Emerald Isle. A year later, I read it in one of the ten volumes of the 'Historiettes' of Tallemant des Réaux, who flourished in the middle of the seventeenth century. The next summer, I happened to choose for my light reading 'Le Moyen de Parvenir,' attributed by most to Beroalde de Varville, although it may possibly be, in part at least, the work of Rabelais; and in this collection, put together in the sixteenth century, again I found my Irish story,—Gascon, this time, I think; certainly no longer Hibernian. It is characteristic of the transmigration of tales, that the story which we find first in the 'Moyen de Parvenir,' avowedly a work of fiction, reappears a hundred years later in the Memoirs of Tallemant as a fact. It is a wise anecdote that knows its own father.

To another French collection, the 'Contes du Sieur Galliard,' by Tabourot des Accords, Mr. Richard Grant White has traced one of the most amusing stanzas of 'Yankee Doodle'—

> Yankee Doodle came to town
>   And wore his striped trowsis;
> Said he couldn't see the town,
>   There were so many houses.

The French ancestor is : "Chascun me disoit que je verrois une si grande et belle ville ; mais on se mocquoit de moi ; car on ne le peut voir à cause de la multitude des maisons qui empêchent la veüe." And I think there is an even older English saying to the effect that one could not see the forest for the trees.

There is no need here to enter on the vexed question of plagiarism, though it is very tempting at all times. One chapter of the ' History of Plagiarism '—another of the interesting books waiting to be written—must contain many facts of interest tending to show the survival of humor. Almost the oldest literary monument in the history of the French comedy is the ' Farce de Maître Pierre Pathelin '; it is as primitive and as positive in its humor as a play can be. An adaptation of it under the name of ' L'Avocat Pathelin ' was made by Brueys and Palaprat, in accordance with the canons of French dramatic art which obtained in the eighteenth century. From 'L'Avocat Pathelin ' was taken an English farce, the ' Village Lawyer,' brought out at Drury Lane under the management of David Garrick. The ' Village Lawyer' kept the stage for nearly a century, and the last time it was acted in New-York Mr. Joseph Jefferson took the chief part. A perversion of the

'Village Lawyer,' under the title of the 'Great Sheep Case,' has been made for the use of the ruder and more boisterous actors who perform in the entertainments known, for some inscrutable reason, as Variety Shows. Thus it happens that one of the earliest comic plays of France still keeps the stage in America—as strong an instance of the tenacity of humor as one could wish.

When a story is authenticated by a proper name we are inclined to treat it with more respect than when it is a mere bastard with no right to a patronymic. There has recently been put into circulation in America an anecdote sharpened to the same point as an anecdote recorded in the histrionic biographies of the last century; but the proper names which appear in both versions lead one to believe that there has been no wilful infringement of copyright. Foote was forever girding at Garrick's parsimony—very unjustly, for Garrick was careful of the pence only that he might have pounds to lend and to give. Garrick dropped a guinea once and sought it in vain, until he gave up the search, saying petulantly, "I believe it has gone to the devil!" Whereupon Foote remarked that Davy could make a guinea go farther than any one else. This is the tale as told in the last century in the Old World. Here is the

1*

tale as told in the New World in this century. When Mr. William M. Evarts was Secretary of State he went with a party to see the Natural Bridge in Virginia, not very far from the capital. Somebody repeated the tradition that George Washington once threw a silver dollar over the bridge—a very remarkable feat of strength and skill. "In those days," was the comment of Mr. Evarts, "in those days a dollar went so much farther than it does now!" Although the point is the same on which the two tales turn, they impress one as of quite independent invention; we may doubt whether Mr. Evarts, who has a merry wit of his own, ever heard of Foote's gibe.

When, however, the story is not vouched for by a proper name, the probability is that the successive reappearances of an anecdote are due to a survival in oral tradition. There is in America a familiar tale, summed up in the phrase "Let the other man walk!" It relates that a traveller in a hotel was kept awake long past midnight by a steady tramp, tramp, tramp, on the floor over him. At last he went upstairs and asked what the matter might be. The occupant of the upper room said that he owed money to another man for which he had given a note, and the note came due on the morrow and he could not meet it.

" Are you certain that you cannot pay your debt?" asked the visitor. " Alas, I cannot," replied the debtor. " Then," said the visitor, " if it cannot be helped, lie down and go to sleep—and let the other man walk!" Now this is a mere Americanization of a story of Poggio's of an inhabitant of Perugia, who walked in melancholy because he could not pay his debts. " Vah, stulte," was the advice given him, " leave anxiety to your creditors!"

Another well-worn American anecdote describes the result of owning both a parrot and a monkey. When the owner of the bird and the beast comes home one day, he finds the monkey decked with red and green feathers, but he does not find the parrot for a long while. At last, the bird appears from an obscure corner plucked bare save a single tail-feather; he hops upon his perch with such dignity as he can muster and says, with infinite pathos, " Oh, we have had a hell of a time!" At first nothing could seem more American than this, but there is a story essentially the same in Walpole's Letters. Yet another parrot story popular in New-York, where a well-known wit happens to be a notorious stutterer, is as little American as this of Walpole's. The stutterer is supposed to ask the man who offers the parrot for

sale if it c–c–c–can t–t–t–talk. "If it could not talk
better than you I'd wring its neck," is the ven-
der's indignant answer. I found this only the
other day in Buckland's 'Curiosities of Natural
History,' first published nearly a quarter of a century ago ; and since this paper was first published
a contributor to the *Dramatic Review* has traced it
back to Henry Philips's 'Recollections.'

The two phrases, "let the other man walk"
and "we have had a hell of a time," have passed
into proverbs in America. The anecdotes in which
they are enshrined happened to tickle the fancy
of the American people most prodigiously. There
is in them, as they are now told in the United
States, a certain dryness and directness and subtlety and extravagance—four qualities characteristic of much of the American humor which is one
of the most abundant of our exports. In nothing
is the note of nationality more distinct than in
jokes. The delicate indelicacies of M. Grévin are
hardly more un-English than the extravagant vagaries of the wild humorists of the boundless prairies
of the West. In Hebrew I am informed and believe the pun is a legitimate figure of lofty rhetoric,
and in England I have observed it is the staple of
comic effort ; in America most of us are intolerant
of the machine-made pun. To be acceptable to

the American mind the pun must have an element
of unexpected depravity—like Dr. Holmes's immortal play on a word when he explains to us that
an onion is like an organ because it smell odious.
As a rule, however, the native American humorist
eschews all mere juggling with double meanings.
He strives to attain an imaginative extravagance,
recalling rather Rabelais than the more decorous
contributors to the collection of *Mr. Punch*. Arte-
mus Ward suggests quietly that it would have
been money in Jeff. Davis's pocket if he had never
been born. Mark Twain in an answer to a correspondent recommends fish as a brain-food, and
after considering the contributions proffered by the
correspondent, indicates as his proper diet two
whales—not necessarily large whales, just ordinary
ones. But one of the best characters Mark Twain
ever sketched from life, Colonel Mulberry Sellers,
is almost exactly like a character in Ben Jonson's
'The Devil is an Ass.' And Charles Lamb and
Sydney Smith would have felt a thrill of delight at
meeting the man who wanted to run up to Rome
from Civita Vecchia that he might have 'twenty
minutes in the Eternal City.' Indeed, if Mark
Twain had only been a parson, he might have
written singularly like unto the merry curate who
once lived five miles from a lemon. Perhaps the

strict theological training would have checked that
tendency to apparent irreverence which leads
Americans to speak disrespectfully of the equator.
I think this irreverence is more apparent than
actual. Americans are brought up on the Bible,
and they use the familiar phrases of the authorized
version without intent of irreverence. I have
seen an Englishman shocked at passages in the
'Biglow Papers' which an American accepted
without hesitation or thought of evil.

Perhaps the most marked of the four chief characteristics of contemporary American humor—
dryness, directness, subtlety, and extravagance—
is a compound of the two latter into something
very closely resembling imagination. An American reviewer of Mr. John Ashton's 'Humor, Wit,
and Satire of the Seventeenth Century'—a most
useful work, by the way, to whosoever shall
undertake hereafter the editing of the 'Authentic
Jest-Book'—drew attention to the unlikeness of
the mere telling of an incident—possibly comic
enough in its happening, but vapid and mirthless
beyond measure when it is set down in cold print
—the unlikeness of this sort of comic tale to the
more imaginative anecdotes now in favor in American newspapers. The reviewer copied from Mr.
Ashton's book a comic tale taken from the 'Sack-

ful of Newes,' published in 1673, and set over
against it•a little bit of the paragraphic humor
which floats hither and thither on the shifting
waves of American journalism. Here is the merry
jest of two centuries ago :

"A certain butcher was flaying a calf at night,
and had stuck a lighted candle upon his head,
because he would be the quicker about his business, and when he had done he thought to take
the same candle to light him to bed ; but he had
forgot where he had set it, and sought about the
house for it, and all the while it stuck in his cap
upon his head and lighted him in seeking it. At
the last one of his fellows came and asked him
what he sought for. 'Marry (quoth he), I look
for the candle which I did flay the calf withal.'
'Why, thou fool,' qd. he, 'thou has a candle in
thy cap.' And then he felt towards his cap, and
took away the candle burning, whereat there was
great laughing and he mocked for his labor, as he
was well worthy."

And here is the journalistic joke of our own day :

"A colored individual who went down on the
slippery flags at the corner of Woodward Avenue
and Congress Street, scrambled up and backed out
into the street, and took a long look towards the
roof of the nearest building.

'You fell from that third-story window!'
remarked a pedestrian who had witnessed the
tumble.

'Boss, I believes yer!' was the prompt reply;
'but what puzzles me am de queshun of how I
got up dar, an' why I was leanin' outer de
winder!'"

Of course neither of these tales would find a
place in the 'Authentic Jest-Book,' for the first is a
flat telling of a flat fact and the second is an obvious invention of the enemy. But they are valuable
as indications of the steady and increasing evolution of humor. Even if the merry jest about the
butcher and his candle had been ennobled by a
great name, it would have gone to the wall as one
of the weakest jokes known to the student of the
history of humor. The doctrine of the survival
of the fittest in the struggle for existence is as
applicable to jests as it is to other entities. A given
joke develops best in a given environment—a
pun, for example, has more chance of life in England, a bit of imaginative extravagance in America,
and a gibe at matrimonial infelicity or infidelity in
France. It would be a great step gained if we
could get at the primordial germs of wit or discover the protoplasm of humor.

Certain jests, like certain myths, exist in variants

in all parts of the world. Comparative mytholo-
gists are diligently collecting the scattered folk-
lore of all races; why should they not also be
gathering together the primitive folk-humor?
Cannot some comparative philologist reconstruct
for us the original jest-book of the Aryan people?
It would be very interesting to know the exact
stock of jokes our forefathers took with them in
their migrations from the mighty East. It would
be most instructive to be informed just how far
they had got in the theory and practice of humor.
It would be a pure joy to discover precisely what
might be the original fund of root-jests laughed at
by Teuton and Latin and Hindoo before these races
were differentiated one from another by time and
travel and climate. I wonder whether the pastoral
Aryan knew and loved an early form of Lamb's
favorite comic tale, the one in which a mad wag
asks the rustic whether that is his own hare or a
wig? And what did the dark-haired Iberian laugh
at before the tall blonde Aryan drove him into the
corners of Europe? It was probably some practical
joke or other, in which a bone knife or a flint
arrow-head played the chief part. The records of
the Semitic race are familiar to us, but we know
nothing or next to nothing about the primitive
humor of the alleged Turanians.

When this good work is well in hand, and when the collector of comic orts and ends is prepared to make his report, there might be held an International Exhibition of Jokes, which would be quite as useful and quite as moral as some of the International Exhibitions we have had of late years. I think I should spend most of my time in the Retrospective Section studying the antique jests. "Old as a circus joke" might be a proverb, and the Christmas pantomime and the Christy Minstrel can supply jokes both practical and otherwise, quite as fatigued and as hoary with age as those of the circus. Among its many advantages this International Exhibition of Jokes would have one of great importance—it would forever dispel the belief in the saying of one of old that there were only thirty-eight good stories in existence, and that thirty-seven of these could not be told before ladies. There might have been some foundation for this saying in the days when the ladies had to leave the table after dinner because the conversation of the gentlemen then became unfit for their ears. While a good joke should be like a pin, in that it should come to a head soon and be able to stand on its point, yet only too many sorry jests are rather to be defined as unlike a mathematical line, in that they have breadth as well as length.

It is perhaps owing to the existence of stories of this sort that woman has lost the faculty of story-telling. Of course, I do not mean that the fair sex are not felicitous at fiction ; the Scheherazades of the serials would confute me at once. I mean that women do not amuse each other by the exchange of anecdote as men are wont to do. They do not retail the latest good thing. They chat, gossip, giggle, converse, talk, and amuse themselves easily together, but they do not swop stories in man-fashion. Where man is objective, woman is subjective. She is satisfied with her own wit, without need of colporting the humor of a stranger. Woman's wit has sex. It is wholly different from man's wit. From Beatrice (though she was said to take hers from the 'C. Merry Tales') to Mrs. Poyser (who gave us that marvellous definition of a conceited man as one who was like the cock that thought the sun rose to hear him crow), the bright women of fiction have been witty rather than humorous. It may be that the distinction between wit and humor is one of sex after all. I have a friend — he is an editor — who declares that the difference between wit and humor, and again between talent and genius, is only the difference between the raspberry and the strawberry. Doubtless God might have made a better berry than the strawberry, and doubtless God

might have given man a better gift than humor—
but he never did. Woman has not the full gift;
she has wit and some humor, it is true, but she
has only a slighter sense of humor, whence comes
much marital unhappiness. As George Eliot tells
us, " a difference of taste in jests is a great strain
of the affections."

It is said that the rustic, both the male and the
female of that peculiar species, has a positive hos-
tility to a new joke. I do not believe this. Of a
certainty it is not true of the American of New
England, who is as humorous in his speech as he
is shrewd in his business dealings, and the more
humor he has the less sharp he is in trade and the
less severe in his views as to the necessity of work.
We may cite in proof of this Mrs. Stowe's delightful portrait of that village ne'er-do-well, Sam Law-
son. And I doubt if it is true of the English rustic
as he really is, for we know it is not true of him as
he appears in the pages of George Eliot and of Mr.
Thomas Hardy. There he has a mother-wit of his
own, and although fond of the old joke, the meaning of which has been fully fathomed, he is not
intolerant of a new quip or a fresh gibe. What he
cannot abide is a variation in the accepted form
of an accepted anecdote. This he will none of—as
a child resolutely rejects the slightest deviation

from the canonical version of the fairy-tale with
which she is fondly familiar. The rustic and the
child are loyal to old friends, whether it be The
Sleeping Beauty in the Woods, or Brer Rabbit and
the Tar-Baby, or Old Grouse in the Gunroom, at
which honest Diggory had laughed these twenty
years, and which now, alas! is utterly lost to the
knowledge of man, even Goldsmith's latest and
most learned biographer confessing perforce that
he has been wholly unable to recover it from out
the darkness of the past.

THE ETHICS OF PLAGIARISM.

HEN Sir Walter Scott came to consider 'Gil Blas,' and the alleged plagiarisms it contains from the Spanish story-tellers, he spoke with the frankness and sturdy sense which were two of his chief characteristics. "Le Sage's claim to originality in this delightful work," he wrote, "has been idly, I had almost said ungratefully, contested by those critics who conceive they detect a plagiarist wherever they see a resemblance in the general subject of the work to one which has been before treated by an inferior artist. It is a favorite theme of laborious dulness to trace out such coincidences; because they appear to reduce genius of the higher order to the usual standard of humanity, and, of course, to bring the author nearer a level with his critics. It is not the mere outline of a story, not even the adopting some details of a former author, which constitutes the literary crime of plagiarism. The proprietor of the pit from whence Chantrey takes his clay might as well pretend to a right in the figure into which it is moulded under his plastic fingers; and the question is in both cases the same — not so much from whom the original substance came, as to whom it owes that which constitutes its real merit and excellence."

In his delightful paper on Gray, Mr. Lowell declares that "we do not ask where people got their hints, but what they made out of them." Mr. Lowell, I doubt me, is speaking for himself alone, and for the few others who attempt the higher criticism with adequate insight, breadth, and equipment. Only too many of the minor critics have no time to ask what an author has done, they are so busy in asking where he may have got his hints. Thus it is that the air is full of accusations of plagiary, and the bringing of these accusations is a disease which bids fair to become epidemic in literary journalism. Perhaps this is a sign, or at least a symptom, of the intellectual decadence of our race which these same critics sometimes venture to announce. In the full flood of a creative period people cannot pause to consider petty charges of plagiarism. Greene's violent outbreak against the only Shakescene of them all, who had decked himself out in their feathers, seems to have excited little or no attention. Nowadays, a pamphlet like Greene's last dying speech and confession would serve as a text for many a leading article and for many a magazine essay.

"There is, I fear," wrote Lord Tennyson to Mr. Dawson, a year or two ago, "a prosaic set growing up among us, editors of booklets, bookworms, index-hunters, or men of great memories and no imagination who impute themselves to the poet, and so believe that he, too, has no imagination, but is forever poking his nose between the pages of some old volumes in order to see what he can appropriate." A pleasant coincidence of thought is to be noted between these words of Lord Tennyson and the remarks of Sir Walter Scott about 'Gil Blas.' Both poets think ill of the laborious dulness of the literary detective, and suggest that he is actuated by malice in judging others by himself. The police detective is akin to the spy, and although his calling is often useful, and perhaps even necessary, we are not wont to choose him as our bosom friend; the amateur literary detective is an almost useless person, who does for pleasure the dirty work by which the real detective gets his bread.

The great feat of the amateur literary detective is to run up parallel columns, and this he can ac-

complish with the agility of an acrobat. When
first invented, the setting of parallel passages side
by side was a most ingenious device, deadly to an
impostor or to a thief caught in the very act of
literary larceny. But these parallel passages must
be prepared with exceeding care, and with the
utmost certainty. Unless the matter on the one
side exactly balance the matter on the other side,
like the packs on a donkey's back, the burden is
likely to fall about the donkey's feet, and he may
chance to break his neck. Parallel columns should
be most sparingly used, and only in cases of absolute necessity. As they are employed now only
too often, they are quite inconclusive ; and it has
been neatly remarked that they are perhaps like
parallel lines, in that they would never meet,
however far produced. Nothing can be more
puerile, childish, infantine even, than the eagerness with which the amateur literary detective
shows, to his own complete satisfaction, that two
of the most original authors who ever wrote—
Shakspere and Molière—were barefaced borrowers
and convicted plagiarists. There are not a few
other of his deeds almost as silly as this. I wonder that the secure ass (the phrase is from the
' Merry Wives of Windsor,' and not mine, I regret
to say) who thinks that Sheridan took his ' Rivals '

from Smollett's 'Humphrey Clinker' and his 'School for Scandal' from his mother's 'Memoirs of Miss Sydney Biddulph '—the absurd persons who have gravely doubted whether Mr. Stevenson did not find the suggestion of his 'Strange Case of Dr. Jekyll and Mr. Hyde' in Hawthorne's 'Dr. Grimshawe's Secret'—and the malicious folk who have been accusing Mr. Haggard with filching the false teeth and lifting the white calves of other African explorers who were not in search of King Solomon's mines—I wonder that the amateur literary detective of this sort has never seen what a strong case can be made out against M. Alphonse Daudet (a notorious imitator of Dickens, it may be remembered) for having extracted the 'Rois en Exile' from the third paragraph of the first chapter of the 'History of Henry Esmond,' and against Mr. Thackeray for having derived this passage from his recollections of a scene in Voltaire's 'Candide.'

It was the original owner of King Solomon's mines who asserted that there was nothing new under the sun; and after the lapse of hundreds of years one may suggest that a ready acceptance of the charge of plagiarism is a sign of low culture, and that a frequent bringing of the accusation is a sign of defective education and deficient intelligence. Almost the first discovery of a student of letters is that the history of literature is little more than a list of curious coincidences.   The folk-tales which lie at the foundation of all fiction are almost the same the wide world over, from the Eskimo at the top of North America to the Zulu at the tip of South Africa; they can hardly have had a common source, and there are few traces of conscious borrowing or of unconscious lending.

These folk-tales are as ancient as they are widespread, and when Uncle Remus relates the adventures of Brer Rabbit and Brer Terrapin, he is repeating a variant of adventures which were told in Greece before Homer sang.   And as these folk-tales were made each by itself and yet alike, in many places and at all ages of the world, so in more formal literature do we find stories strangely similar one to another, and yet independently invented.   People have always been ready, like the Athenians of old, to hear or to tell some new thing—and the new thing, when dissected, is soon seen to be an old thing.   The tales have all been told.   If we were to take from the goodman La Fontaine the *contes* which had had another owner before he found them by the highway, he would be left like a Manx cat or the flock of Little Bo-Peep.   There are some situations, primitive and powerful, which recur in all literatures with

the inevitable certainty of the fate which domi-
nates them.   What is the 'Hamlet' of Shakspere,
in its essence, but the 'Orestes' trilogy of Æschy-
lus?   And what man shall be bold enough to claim
for himself or for another the first use of the Hidden
Will, of the Infants-changed-at-Nurse, or of the
Stern-Parent-who-cuts-off-his-Son-with-a-Shilling?

After recording a slight similarity of subject and
of point of view between the 'Famille Benoiton'
of M. Victorien Sardou and the 'Young Mrs. Win-
throp' of Mr. Bronson Howard, Mr. William
Archer remarks pertinently that " in the domain
of the drama there is no such thing as private
property in the actual soil ; all that the playwright
can demand is security for his improvements," and
he adds that " were tenure in fee-simple permis-
sible, the whole cultivable area would long ago
have been occupied by a syndicate of pestilent
land-grabbers, named Menander, Calderon, Shakspere & Co., and the dramatist of to-day would
have had no resource save emigration to some
other planet."   I have read that Schiller in the last
century, and Scribe in this, made out a list of all
the possible dramatic situations, and that both lists
were surprisingly brief.   M. Zola's admirable definition of art is " Nature seen through a temperament " ; and the most a man may bring nowadays

is his temperament, his personal equation, his own pair of spectacles, through which he may study the passing show in his own way.

As it is with situations which are the broad effects of the drama or the novel or the poem, so it is with the descriptions and the dialogue which make the smaller effects. Words are more abundant than situations, but they are wearing out with hard usage. Language is finite, and its combinations are not countless. "It is scarcely possible for any one to say or write anything in this late time of the world to which, in the rest of the literature of the world, a parallel could not be found somewhere," so Lord Tennyson declared in the letter from which I have already quoted. "Are not human eyes all over the world looking at the same objects, and must there not consequently be coincidences of thought and impressions and expressions?" The laureate was not at all surprised to be told that there were two lines in a certain Chinese classic (of which he had never heard) exactly like two of his. Once I found an exceedingly close translation of one of Lord Tennyson's lines in a French comedy in verse, and when I asked the dramatist about it, I soon saw that he did not know anything about the English poem,—or even about the English poet.

In cases like these there is no need to dispute the good faith of the author who may chance to be later in point of time. " When a person of fair character for literary honesty uses an image such as another has employed before him, the presumption is that he has struck upon it independently, or unconsciously recalled it, supposing it his own," said the Autocrat of the Breakfast Table. After this dictum in ethics, Dr. Holmes enunciated a subtle psychologic truth, which is known to all conscientious writers, and which should be made known to all amateur literary detectives : " It is impossible to tell, in a great many cases, whether a comparison which suddenly suggests itself is a new conception or a recollection. I told you the other day that I never wrote a line of verse that seemed to me comparatively good but it appeared old at once, and often as if it has been borrowed." Sheridan bears witness to the same effect in the preface to the 'Rivals,' when he says that " faded ideas float in memory like half-forgotten dreams ; and the imagination in its fullest enjoyments becomes suspicious of its offspring, and doubts whether it has created or adopted." Perhaps the testimony of Sheridan is not altogether beyond suspicion ; he had an easy conscience and a marvellous faculty of assimilation, and it may be that

he was apologetically making the plea of confession and avoidance, as the lawyers call it.
But I think that Lord Tennyson, Sir Walter Scott,
and Mr. Lowell are unimpeachable witnesses. It
is with malice prepense that I have quoted from
them frequently and at length, and perhaps in
excess, that I might establish my case not out of
my own mouth, but out of theirs.

After all, there is little need to lay stress on the
innocence of many if not most of the coincidences
with which the history of literature is studded.
The garden is not large, and those who cultivate it
must often walk down the same path, sometimes
side by side, and sometimes one after another,
even though the follower neither wishes nor in-
tends to tread on his predecessor's heels or to
walk in his footsteps. They may gather a nose-
gay of the same flowers of speech. They may
even pluck the same passion-flower, not knowing
that any one has ever before broken a blossom
from that branch. Indeed, when we consider
how small the area is, how few are the possible
complications of plot, how easily the poetic vocabulary is exhausted, the wonder is really, not that
there are so many parallel passages, but that there
are so few. In the one field which is not circum-
scribed there is very little repetition : human

nature is limitless, and characters comparatively rarely pass from one book to another. The dramatists and the romancers have no choice but to treat anew as best they may the well-worn incidents and the weary plots; the poets happen on the same conceits generation after generation; but the dramatists and the romancers and the poets know that there is no limit to the variety of man, and that human nature is as deep and as boundless and as inexhaustible as the ocean. No matter how heavy a draft Shakspere and Molière may have made, no matter how skilfully and how successfully Dickens and Thackeray may have angled, no matter how great the take of Hawthorne and Poe, there are still as good fish in the sea of humanity as ever were caught. And I offer this fact, that we do not find the coincidence in character which we cannot help seeing in plot and in language, as a proof that most apparent plagiarism is quite unconscious and due chiefly to the paucity of material.

Hitherto I have considered only the similarity which was unconscious. Originality is difficult; it is never accidental; and it is to be obtained only by solitary confinement and hard labor. To make his fiction out of whole cloth, to spin his net, spider-like, out of himself, is one of the highest

achievements of the intellect. Only a rare genius
may do this, and he must do it rarely. A man
may always draw from the common stock without
compunction, and there are many circumstances
under which he may borrow unhesitatingly from
other authors. For example, Mr. Haggard has
recently been encompassed about by a cloud of
false witnesses, accusing him of having plagiarized
certain episodes of his story, 'King Solomon's
Mines,' from a certain book of travels. He promptly denied the charge, and of course it fell to the
ground at once. But had he done what he was
accused of doing, there would have been no harm
in it. Mr. Haggard, in writing a romance of Africa,
would have been perfectly justified in using the
observations and experiences of African travellers.
Facts are the foundation of fiction, and the novelist
and the romancer, the dramatist and the poet, may
make free with labors of the traveller, the historian, the botanist, and the astronomer. Within
reason, the imaginative author may help himself
to all that the scientific author has stored up. One
might even go so far as to say that science—in
which I include history—exists to supply facts for
fiction, and that it has not wholly accomplished its
purpose until it has been transmuted in the imagination of the poet. If Mr. Haggard had made

2*

use of a dozen books of African travel in the composition of that thrilling and delightful romance of
adventure, 'King Solomon's Mines,' there would
have been no more taint of plagiary about it than
there was in Shakspere's reworking of the old
chronicles into his historical plays.

Shakspere and Molière borrowed from Plautus,
as Plautus had borrowed from Menander; and this
again is not plagiarism. Every literary worker has
a right to draw from the accumulated store of the
past, so long as he does not attempt to conceal
what he has done nor to take credit for what is not
his own invention, and so long as he has wholly
absorbed and assimilated and steeped in his own
gray matter what he has derived from his predecessors. The elder Dumas has told us how he
found some of the scattered elements of his virile
and vigorous drama 'Henri III.' in Anquetil and in
Scott and in Schiller; but the play is his, none the
less; and this was no plagiarism, for he had mixed
himself, with what he borrowed, "an incalculable
increment," as Mr. Lowell said of Gray. 'Henri III.'
lives with its own life, which Dumas gave it, and
which is as different as possible from the life of
the fragments of Anquetil, Scott, and Schiller, each
of these again differing one from the other. It
was as unlike as may be to that merely literary

imitation which Hawthorne compared to a plaster cast.

Another French dramatist, M. Sardou, had profited by the reading of Poe's 'Purloined Letter' when he sat down to plan his 'Pattes de Mouche'; but it is absurd to talk of plagiary here, and to call M. Sardou's charming comedy a dramatization of Poe's short story, for, although the bare essential idea is the same, the development is radically different. And in like manner Poe found an incident in Mr. Mudford's 'Iron Shroud' which probably suggested to him his own appalling tale of the 'Pit and the Pendulum.' Here what Poe took from Mr. Mudford was very little compared with what he contributed himself; and in any discussion of plagiarism quite the most important question is the relative value to the borrower of the thing borrowed. If he has flocks of his own, he may lift the ewe lamb of his neighbor, and only laborious dulness will object. The plagiarist, in fact, is the man who steals his brooms ready made, because he does not know how to make them. Dumas and M. Sardou and Poe were men having a highly developed faculty of invention, and seeking originality diligently. Those from whom they borrowed have no more right to claim the resulting works than has the spectator who lends a coin to a

conjurer a right to consider himself a partner in the
ingenious trick the conjurer performs with it. If
this be plagiary, make the most of it. Let us all
wish for more of it. And this reminds me of a
little story, as Lincoln used to say: in the darkest
days of our war, when defeat followed defeat, and
Grant alone was victorious at Vicksburg, some
busybody went to Lincoln and told him that Grant
drank whiskey. "Does he?" said the President,
gravely. "Do you happen to know what kind of
whiskey it is? Because I should like to send a
barrel of it to some of the other generals."

"Far indeed am I from asserting that books, as
well as nature, are not, and ought not to be, suggestive to the poet," wrote Lord Tennyson. "I am
sure that I myself and many others find a peculiar
charm in those passages of such great masters as
Virgil or Milton, where they adopt the creation of
a bygone poet, and reclothe it, more or less, according to their fancy." Wordsworth said that
Gray helped himself from everybody and every-
where; but what Gray made out of these old bits
borrowed from others was a new poem, and it was
his own. In the latest editions of Gray's poems, as
Mr. Lowell has put it picturesquely, "The thin line
of text stands at the top of the page like cream,
and below it is the skim-milk drawn from many

milky mothers of the herd out of which it has risen." It was because the author of 'Evangeline' followed the example of the author of the 'Elegy' that Poe was able to write his foolish paper on 'Mr. Longfellow and other Plagiarists'—a wanton attack which Longfellow bore with beautiful serenity. One must set a plagiarist to cry " Stop thief!" and Poe was not above stealing his brooms, or at least his smaller brushes, ready made. We may absolve him for levying on Mudford for the 'Pit and the Pendulum,' but in his ' Marginalia' he retailed as his own Sheridan's joke about the phœnix and Whitbread's poulterer's description of it.

I believe that both Ben Jonson and the elder Dumas defended their forays into the marches of their elders, and even of their contemporaries, by the bold assertion that genius does not steal, it conquers. And there is force in the plea. Genius takes by right of eminent domain, and rectifies its frontier by annexing outlying territory, making fruitful that which before was but a barren waste. In literature, that is his at last who makes best use of it. And here is the essence of the controversy in a nutshell : it is plagiarism for an author to take anything from another author and reproduce it nakedly ; but it is not necessarily plagiarism if he reclothes it and dresses it up anew. If the second comer can improve on the work of the first comer, if he makes it over and makes it better, and makes it his own, we accept the result and ask no questions. But if he make no change, or if he make a change for the worse, we send for the police at once. A man may be allowed to keep his borrowed brats, if he clothe them and feed them and educate them, and if he make no attempt to disguise them, and if he is not guilty of the fatal mistake of disfiguring them " as the gypsies do stolen children to make 'em pass for their own." (This figure, by the way, was an orphan of Churchill's when Sheridan came along and adopted it.) Thus, we find it hard to forgive Herrick for one of his thefts from Suckling, when he took the loveliest lines of the lovely ' Ballad upon a Wedding' :

> Her feet beneath her petticoat,
> Like little mice, stole in and out,
> As if they feared the light,

and in his ' Hesperides' he spoilt them to

> Her pretty feet, like snails, did creep a little out.

Nothing is further from my desire than that I should be taken either as a defender of plagiarism or as a denier of its existence. It exists, and it is

an ugly crime.   What I am seeking to show is
that it is not as frequent as many may imagine,
and more especially that much which is called
plagiarism is not criminal at all, but perfectly
legitimate.   For instance, Mr. Charles Reade's in-
corporation of fragments of the 'Dialogues' of
Erasmus in the 'Cloister and the Hearth,' and of
Swift's 'Polite Conversation' in the 'Wandering
Heir,' was a proper and even a praiseworthy use
of preëxisting material.   But Mr. Reade did not
always remain within his rights, and it is impossible to doubt that his 'Portrait' was first
hung in the private gallery of Mme. Reybaud,
and that some of his 'Hard Cash' was filched
from the coffers of the 'Pauvres de Paris' of
MM. Brisebarre and Nus.   Mme. Reybaud's picture was not a Duchess of Devonshire which a
man might so fall in love with that he could
not help stealing it — indeed, it is not easy to
discover why Mr. Reade wanted it; but the
drama of MM. Brisebarre and Nus is ingeniously
pathetic, and although no one has made as skilful use of its fable as Mr. Reade, it has served
to suggest also Miss Braddon's 'Rupert God-
win, Banker,' Mr. Sterling Coyne's 'Fraud and
its Victims,' and Mr. Dion Boucicault's 'Streets of
New-York.'

It is in the theatre that we hear the most accusations of plagiarism.   Apparently there is an un-
willingness on the part of the public to believe
that a play can be original, and a dramatist
nowadays is forced not only to affirm his innocence, but almost to prove it.   I am inclined
to think that the habit of adapting from the
French—a habit now happily in its decline—is
responsible for this state of things, for the laxity
of morals on the part of the author, and for the
general and ungenerous suspicion on the side of
the public.

It is the playwright's fault, one must confess, if
the playgoer is doubtful as to the paternity of every
new play.   So many pieces were brought out as
"new and original," which were neither original
nor new, that the playgoer was confirmed in his
suspicions; and he finds it hard to surrender the
habit of doubt even now when a French drama in
an English or American theatre generally bears the
French author's name, and when the best work of
the best English and American dramatists is really
their own.   Mr. Herman Merivale and Mr. Bronson
Howard, Mr. Gilbert and Mr. Pinero, and other of
the little band of young playmakers whose work
seems to promise a possible revival of the English
drama as a form of art and a department of litera-

ture, are quite above the meanness of taking a foreign author's plot without authority or acknowledgment. Yet they suffer for the sins of their predecessors.

Credit, said a great economist, is suspicion asleep; and the saying is as true in the playmaking profession as it is in the trade of moneymaking. Suspicion is suffering from an acute attack of insomnia just now, and many dramatic critics are quick to declare a resemblance between Macedon and Monmouth, if there be salmons in both, and when the dramatist is shown to have lifted a tiny lamb they are ready to hang him for a stalwart sheep. Now, there is no department of literature in which similarities are as inevitable as they are in the drama. I have tried to show already that the elements of the drama are comparatively few, and that the possible combinations are not many. There are only a few themes suited for treatment in the theatre, and many a topic which a novelist can handle to advantage the dramatist is debarred from attempting by the conditions of the stage. A certain likeness there must needs be between the new plays and the old plays in which the same subject has been discussed by the dramatist. And these coincidences may be as innocent as they are "curious."

I remember that when Mr. Dion Boucicault originally produced the 'Shaughraun'—it was at Wal-
lack's Theatre in New-York ten or twelve years
ago—there was an attempt to prove that he had
taken his plot from an earlier Irish drama by Mr.
Wybert Reeve. At first sight the similarity between
the two plays was really striking, and parallel columns were erected with ease. But a closer investigation revealed that all that was common to these
two plays was common to fifty other Irish plays,
and that all that gave value to the 'Shaughraun'—
the humor, the humanity, the touches of pathos,
the quick sense of character—was absent from the
other play.   There is a formula for the mixing of
an Irish drama, and Mr. Reeve and Mr. Boucicault
had each prepared his piece according to this
formula, making due admixture of the Maiden-in-
Distress, the Patriot-in-danger-of-his-Life, and the
Cowardly Informer, who have furnished forth
many score plays since first the Red-Coats were
seen in the Green Isle. Both dramatists had drawn
from the common stock of types and incidents,
and there was really no reason to believe that Mr.
Boucicault was indebted to Mr. Reeve for anything,
because Mr. Reeve had little in his play which had
not been in twenty plays before, and which Mr.
Boucicault could not have put together out of his

recollections of these without any knowledge of that. Of course there is a great difference between the original and the commonplace, but if a man cannot be the former it is no sin to be the latter. Commonplace is not plagiarism. That a coat is threadbare is no proof that it has been stolen—on the contrary.

To any one understanding the subtlety of mental processes, and especially the movements of the imagination, a similarity of situation is often not only not a proof of plagiarism, but a proof that there has been no plagiarism. This sounds like a paradox, but I think I can make my meaning clear and evident. When we find the same strikingly original idea differently handled by two authors, we may absolve the later from any charge of literary theft if we find that his treatment of the novel situation differs from his predecessor's. If the treatment is different, we may assume that the second writer was not aware of the existence of the first writer's work. And for this reason: if the later author were acquainted with the startlingly novel effect of the earlier author, he could not have treated the same subject without repeating certain of the minor peculiarities also. He must perforce have taken over with the theme in some measure the treatment also. All literary workmen know how difficult it is to disentangle the minor details from the main idea, and to strip the idea naked, discarding the mere detail. Had the second writer known of the first writer's work, he could not help being influenced by it. Thus it is that a similarity of subject may be evidence of originality. There is a short story by FitzJames O'Brien, called 'What Was It?' in which there is a palpable but invisible being. Since this was first published there have been two other short stories on the same idea, one published in the *Atlantic Monthly* by Mr. Charles de Kay, and the other published anonymously in the *Cornhill Magazine*. The tale in the *Cornhill* coincides in detail as well as in idea, and it is almost impossible to declare its anonymous author guiltless of plagiarism. But Mr. de Kay's story was wholly different in its elaboration, and the two tales, although the chief figure in each was a being palpable but invisible, were as unlike as possible. Here there was obviously no plagiarism. The coat — to take up the figure of the last paragraph — was made of the same cloth, but its cut was not the same.

(Lately — since this paper first appeared — the central figure of FitzJames O'Brien's story has been seen again in 'Le Horla' of M. Guy de Maupassant, but with a treatment so personal and a

modification so striking that it seems impossible
that the French author has not happened on it independently,—however easy it might be to prepare parallel columns to prove him a plagiarist.)

Three or four years ago the *Saturday Review*
laid down the law of plagiarism in three clauses :
1. "In the first place, we would permit any great
modern artist to recut and to set anew the literary
gems of classic times and of the Middle Ages."
2. "Our second rule would be that all authors
have an equal right to the stock situations which
are the common store of humanity." 3. "Finally,
we presume that an author has a right to borrow
or buy an idea, if he frankly acknowledges the
transaction." In commenting on this code, I suggested that there might be a difficulty of interpre-
tation in the first clause, for who is to declare any
modern a great artist? In the second clause the
law is clearly stated, and whether any given situation is or is not common property is a question of
fact for the jury. The only difficulty in applying
the third clause is in defining precisely the degree
of frankness and fulness required in acknowledg-
ing the indebtedness. But hypercriticism is out
of place in considering a suggestion as valuable, as
needful just now, and as neatly put up as this
triple law of the contributor to the *Saturday*

Review. A general acceptance of this code would tend to clear the air of the vague charges of plagiarism which hang in heavy clouds over the literary journals. Before we can decide whether an author is guilty of the offence, we must be agreed on what constitutes the crime, what are its elements, and what are the exemptions. I have ventured to draw up the statute of exemptions in a form slightly different from that given in the *Saturday Review*, a little broader and stronger, and perhaps a little simpler : A writer is at liberty to use the work of his predecessors as he will, provided always that (1) he does not take credit (even by implication) for what he has not invented, and (2) that he does not in any way infringe on the pecuniary rights of the original owner.

When M. Sardou brought out the farcical comedy 'Les Pommes du Voisin,' he was accused of having stolen it from a tale of Charles de Bernard, and he retorted instantly with evidence that he had the permission of the holders of the Bernard copyrights, who were to share in the profits of the play. Here M. Sardou was innocent under the second clause of my law, but guilty under the first, insomuch as he had concealed his indebtedness to Charles de Bernard and had taken credit for an invention which was not his own. When

Mr. Charles Reade turned Mrs. Burnett's 'That Lass o' Lowrie's' into a play called 'Joan,' without asking the permission of the American author, he was guilty under the second clause and innocent under the first, for there was no concealment of the source of the drama.

With a proper understanding of what is and what is not plagiarism, there should go a greater circumspection in bringing the accusation. Plagiarism is the worst of literary crimes. It is theft, neither more nor less. All who desire to uphold the honor of literature, and to see petty larceny and highway robbery meet with their just punishment, are concerned that the charge shall not be idly brought or carelessly answered. But now so often has the amateur literary detective cried "Wolf" that patience is exhausted, and accusations of literary theft have been flung broadcast, until they may be met with a smile of contempt. This is not as it should be. It is contrary to public policy that the literary conscience should become callous. The charge of plagiarism is very serious, and it should not be lightly brought or lightly borne. The accusation is very easy to make and very hard to meet; it should be a boomerang, which, when skilfully thrown, brings down the quarry with a single deadly blow, but which,

when carelessly cast, rebounds swiftly and breaks
the head of him who threw it. The man who
makes the charge of plagiarism should be ready
to stand to his guns, and to pay the penalty of
having opened fire. And the penalty for having
failed to prove the accusation should be heavy.
The accuser should be put under bonds, so to
speak, to make his charge good, and if he loses his
case he should be cast in damages. It is not right
to force an author either unjustly to lie under an
accusation of theft, or to undergo the annoyance
and expense of refuting vague allegations, urged
in wanton carelessness by some irresponsible person. Nothing is more disagreeable or thankless
than a dispute with an inferior. Years ago Dr.
Holmes declared the hydrostatic paradox of controversy: "Controversy equalizes fools and wise
men in the same way—and the fools know it!"

If we were to hold to a strict accountability the
feeble-minded persons who delight in pointing out
alleged coincidences and similarities, if we were to
discourage the accusation of plagiarism, except on
abundant evidence, if we were to declare that
any man who fails to sustain his charge shall be
discredited, we should do much to put down
plagiarism itself. When the difficulties and the
dangers of making the accusation are increased—

and it is now neither difficult nor dangerous—the number of accusations will be decreased at once, and in time the public conscience will be quickened. Then it would be possible to get serious attention for the serious case of literary theft, and then the writer who might be found with stolen wares concealed about his person would be visited with swifter condemnation and with more certain punishment.   But now all we can do is to remember that

The man who plants cabbages imitates too.

THE TRUE THEORY OF THE PREFACE —

A Confidential Communication to all Makers of Books.

PPARENTLY the true theory of the Preface is apprehended by very few of those who are, by trade, makers of books—to use Carlyle's characterization of his own calling. Mr. Matthew Arnold, indeed, master of all literary arts, was highly skilful in the use of the Preface, which, in his hands, served to drive home the bolt of his argument, and to rivet it firmly on the other side. Those who have read one of Mr. Arnold's prefaces know what to expect, and fall to, with increased appetite, on the book itself. But not many men may wield the weapons of Mr. Arnold, and very few, as I have hinted already, are skilled in the use of the Preface. Many, ignorant of its utility, choose to ignore it altogether. More, accepting it as a necessary evil, acquit themselves of it in the most perfunctory fashion. There is slight survival of the tradition which made the appeal to the Gentle Reader a fit and proper custom.   But nowadays the appeal is useless, and the Gentle Reader—oh, where is he?   In the days when there was a Gentle Reader there was no giant critic to appal the trembling author with his thunderous Fee-Fo-Fum.   In the beginning, when printing was a new invention, it served for the multiplication of books alone ; newspapers lagged long after ; and it is only in the present century that the reading public began to allow that middle-man, the critic, to taste and try before they buy. The Preface *in formâ pauperis,* in which the author confessed his sinful publication and implored forgiveness, urging as his sole excuse " hunger and request of friends," is now as much out of date and as antiquated in style as the fulsome dedication to a noble patron.   The two lived together and died together about the time when the working man of letters moved out of his lodgings in Grub Street.

The Preface in which the writer takes a humorous view of his own work is a late device ; it is capable of good results in the hands of a literary artist like Mr. Robert Louis Stevenson, who suggests in the pages which prepare us to enjoy his record of ' An Inland Voyage ' that in his Preface an author should stand afar off and look at his book affectionately, if he will, but dispassionately. "It is best, in such circumstances," he asserts, "to represent a delicate shade of manner between humility and superiority, as if the book had been written by some one else, and you had merely run over it and inserted what was good." Clever as this is, and characteristic and delightful as its humor is, I feel constrained to assert my belief that Mr. Stevenson is not standing on the solid ground of a sound theory. Mr. Stevenson is a writer of exceptional gifts, and he may venture on liberties which would be fatal to the rest of us: his example affords no safe rule for ordinary mortals. In the Preface a man must take himself seriously, for a Preface is a very serious thing. It cannot be denied that the humorous attitude is much wiser than the self-depreciatory and the apologetic, which are, unfortunately, far more common. A humorist has, at least, a wholesome belief in himself, and he can hide his doubting sorrow with a smile; whereas the plaintive author, who confesses his weakness with tears in his eyes, is a sorry spectacle that no critic need respect.

The cause of the apologetic Preface is obvious enough. Although printed at the beginning of the book, the Preface is the final thing written. When the long labor of composition is over at

last, and the intense strain is relaxed suddenly,
then it is that the author sits down to his Preface.
There is a cooling of the enthusiasm which has
carried him through his work ; there is often,
indeed, a violent reaction ; and it is at this moment of depression and despondency, when the
writer is a prey to dread doubt about his book and
about himself, that the Preface has to be composed.
Just then the author sometimes wonders whether
it is not his duty to throw what he has written into the fire, and so rid the world of a misconceived
and misshapen abortion.   Rarely is this feeling,
acute as it is, and painful, quite strong enough to
make the author actually cast his MS. into the
grate—never until, like Pendennis, he has made
sure that the fire is out.   But his morbidity of spirit
and his self-distrust find vent in the Preface.   Not
unfrequently is the Preface worded like a last
dying speech and confession.   As M. Octave Uz-
anne says in the lively Preface to his lively little
book called the ' Caprices d'un Bibliophile,' " the
Preface is the salutation to the reader, and too
often, alas ! the terrible salutation of the gladiators
to Cæsar—*Morituri te salutant !* "

This is rank heresy : and all such heretics should
be burnt at the stake, or at least they should have
their books burnt in the market-place by the com-

mon hangman. The Preface is not the fit time
and occasion for the author to exhale his plaints,
to make confession of his sins, and to promise to
do penance. It is perhaps not too much to say that
the Preface is the most important part of a book,
except the Index. Anybody can write a book,
such as it is, but only a gifted man, or a man
trained in the art, can write a Preface, such as it
ought to be.

In the Preface the author must put his best foot
foremost, and this is often the *premier pas qui
coûte*. A Preface should be appetizing, alluring,
enticing. As a battle well joined is half-won, as a
work well begun is half-done, so a book with a
good Preface is half-way on the high-road to success. In the Preface the author offers his first-
fruits and pours his libation. In the Preface the
author sets a sample of his text as in a show-
window. In the Preface the author strikes the
key-note of his work. Therefore must the good
Preface set forth the supreme excellence of the
book it should precede, as a brass-band goes
before a regiment. As delicately, and yet as unhesitatingly, as the composer knows how, the
Preface should sound triumphant pæans of exult-
ant self-praise. There is no need that a Preface
should be long ; it takes a large cart to carry a

score of empty casks, almost worthless, while a ten-thousand-dollar diamond may go snugly in a waistcoat-pocket.   But a Preface must be strong enough to do its allotted work.   Now, its allotted work — and here we are laying bare the secret of the true theory of the Preface — is to furnish to the unwitting critic a syllabus or a skeleton of the criticism which you wish to have him write.

The thoughtless may declare that "nobody reads a Preface"; but there could be no more fatal blunder.   Perhaps that impalpable entity, the general reader, may skip it not infrequently; but that tangible terror, the critic, never fails to read the Preface, even when he reads no farther.   Now and again the general reader may dispense with the reading of the Preface, as legislative assemblies dispense with the reading of the minutes of the last meeting, that they may the sooner get to the business in hand.   The critic is a very different sort of person from the general reader, and it is meat and drink to him to read a Preface.   The author should recognize this fact; he should accept the altered conditions of the Preface.   Consider for a moment what the Preface was, what it is now, and what it should be.   It was addressed to the reader, who read it rarely.   It is now, as we have seen above, anything or nothing, sometimes absent, often artless, seldom apt. It should be a private letter from the author to the critic indicating the lines upon which he (the author) would like him (the critic) to frame an opinion and to declare a judgment. A good Preface is like the trick modern magicians use, when, under pretence of giving us free choice, they force us to draw the card they have already determined upon. So if a book have a proper Preface, contrived with due art, the critic cannot choose but write about it as the author wishes. A master of the craft will blow his own horn in the Preface of his book so skilfully and so unobtrusively that only a faint echo shall linger in the ear of the critic, iterating and reiterating the *Leit-Motiv* of self-praise until the charmed reviewer repeats it unconsciously.

Of course it is not easy for a gentleman to praise himself publicly as he feels he deserves to be praised. The pleasantest and most profitable Preface for the beginner in book-making is the introduction by one of the acknowledged leaders of literature. Then, by a strange reversal of custom, it is the celebrity who waits at the door like an usher to declare the titles of the young man who is about to cross the threshold for the first time. Thus the young author has granted to him a passport by which he may gain admittance where else

he might not enter. Jules Janin was a master-
hand at the issuing of these introductory letters of
credit ; he was easy and good-natured, and rarely
or never did he refuse a novice the alms of a Preface. Janin had the ear of the public, and he liked
to lead the public by the ear. Perhaps, too, he
liked the opportunity of using his high praise of
the new-comer slyly to deal a blow between the
ribs or under the belt of some old favorite whose
reputation came between him and the sun. He
who makes the Preface to another's book stands
on a vantage-ground and is free from responsi-
bility ; he may classify under heads the things that
he hates, and then, in accordance with the precept
and the practice of Donnybrook, hit a head where-
ever he sees it. Truly a man may wish, "O that
mine enemy would let me write his Preface!
Could I not damn with faint praise and stab with
sharp insinuendo?"— to use the labor-saving and
much-needed word thoughtlessly invented by the
sable legislator of South Carolina.

The Preface by another hand is often a pleasant
device for the display of international courtesy.
Merimée introduced Turgenef to the Parisians. In
the United States an English author may be presented to the public by an American celebrity, and
in Great Britain an American book may be pub-

3*

lished with a voucher of its orthodoxy signed by a
dignitary of the Church. The exalted friend of the
author who provides the introduction, if he be but
a true friend, may praise far more highly than even
the wiliest author would dare to praise himself.
If he understands the obligation of his position and
does his duty, he should blare the trumpet boldly
and bang the big-drum mightily, and bid the
whole world walk up and see the show which is
just about to begin. Even if the public be dull
and laggard and refuse to be charmed, the author
has at least the signal satisfaction for once in his
life of hearing his effort properly appreciated at its
exact value. If by any chance he is a truly modest
man — a rare bird indeed, a white black-bird — he
may have some slight qualms of conscience on
seeing himself over-praised in the pages of his own
book. But these qualms are subdued easily
enough for the most part. "I never saw an
author in my life — saving perhaps one," says the
Autocrat, "that did not purr as audibly as a full-
grown domestic cat on having his fur smoothed
the right way by a skilful hand."

In default of a friend speaking as one having
authority, the author must perforce write his own
Preface and declare his own surpassing virtues.
The old-fashioned Preface, inscribed to the Gentle

Reader of the vague and doubtful past, often failed to reach its address.   The Preface of the new school, constructed according to the true theory, is intended solely for the critic.   Now, the critic is the very reverse of the Gentle Reader, and he must be addressed accordingly.   He studies the Preface carefully to see what bits he can chip away to help build his own review.   " A good Preface is as essential to put the reader into good humor as a good prologue to a play," so the author of the 'Curiosities of Literature' tells us; but nowadays our plays have no prologues, and it is the critic whom the Preface must put into good humor. Now, the critic is not the ogre he is often represented ; he is a man like ourselves, a man having to earn his bread by the sweat of his brow, a man often over-worked and often bound down to a distasteful task.   He is quick to take a hint.   For his benefit the Preface should fairly bristle with hints.   The Preface should insinuate adroitly that the book it precedes is — in the choice phrase of the advertisement — " a felt-want filled."   This need not be done brutally and nakedly.   On the contrary, it is better to lead the mind of the critic by easy steps. Dwell on the importance of the subject, and declare that in the present work it has been regarded for the first time from a new and particular point of view. Point out, modestly but firmly, the special advantages which the author has enjoyed, and which make him an authority on the subject. Casually let drop, in quotation marks, a few words of high praise once addressed to the author by a great man, now no longer with us, and trust that you have done all in your power to merit such gratifying encomiums. You may even venture to intimate that although you cannot expect the profane vulgar to see the transcendent merit of your work, yet the favored few of keener insight will recognize it at once: flattery is a legal-tender without Act of Congress, and the critic accepts it as readily, perhaps, as the author. The critic is only a fellow human being after all, and like the rest of our fellow human beings he is quite ready to take us at our own valuation. Hold the head up; look the world in the eye; and he is a churlish critic who does not at least treat you with respect.

But if the Preface is weak in tone, if it is nerveless, if it is apologetic, then the critic takes the author at his word and has a poor opinion of him, and expresses that opinion in plain language. If you throw yourself on the mercy of the court, the critic gives you at once the full penalty of the law. Confess a lamb and the critic hangs you for a sheep. Give him but five lines of Preface

and he can damn any book. Acknowledge any
obligation, however slight, and the critic pounces
upon it ; and your character for originality is lost.
Every admission will be used against you. He believes that you undervalue your indebtedness to
others ; and if you rashly call his attention to it, he
tries to balance the account by overstating your
debt. I know an author who had studied a subject for years, contributing from time to time to
periodicals an occasional paper on certain of its
sub-divisions, until at last he was ready to write
his book about it ; his honesty moved him to say
in the Preface of the volume that he had made use
of articles in certain magazines and reviews. He
did not specifically declare that these articles were
his own work, and so one critic called the book "a
compilation from recent periodical literature," leav-
ing the reader to infer that the author had been
caught decking himself out in borrowed plumes.
Two friends of the same author kindly consented
to read the proof-sheets of another of his books ;
and in the Preface thereof he thanked them by
name for "the invaluable aid they have kindly
given me in the preparation of these pages for the
press." One critic took advantage of this acknowledgment to credit the two friends with a material
share in the work of which they had only read the

proof. The author of that remarkable book, the 'Story of a Country Town,' wrote a most pathetic Preface, a cry of doubt wrung from his heart; and there was scarcely a single favorable review of the volume the praise of which had not been dampened by the Preface.

The only safe rule is resolutely to set forth the merits of the book in the Preface, and to be silent as to its faults. Do not apologize for anything. Confess nothing. If there are omissions, pride yourself on them. If the book has an inevitable defect, boast of it. A man has the qualities of his faults, says the French maxim; in a Preface, a man must defiantly set up his faults as qualities. Of course this needs to be done with the greatest skill; and it is seen in perfection only in the Prefaces of those who have both taste and tact, and who combine a masculine vigor of handling with a feminine delicacy of touch. Anybody can write a book,— as I have said already,— but only a man singularly gifted by nature and richly cultivated by art can write a Preface as it ought to be written.

If common decency requires absolutely that the author confess something, an indebtedness to a predecessor, or the like, even then this confession must not encumber and disfigure the Preface. Dismiss the thought of the confession wholly from

your mind while you are composing the Preface.
Then declare your indebtedness and avow any of
the seven deadly sins of which you may have been
guilty — in a note, in a modest and unobtrusive
little note, either at the end of the book or at the
bottom of the page.   The critic always reads the
Preface, but only a man really interested in the
subject ever digs into a note. A foot-note, lurking
shyly in fine type, is perhaps the best place for a
man to confess his sins in.   And yet there is a
great advantage in postponing the bad quarter of
an hour as long as possible — that is to say, to the
very end of the book.   When the aspiring dramatist brought his tragedy to Sheridan as the manager of Drury Lane, he said that he had written the
prologue himself and he had ventured to hope that
perhaps Mr. Sheridan would favor him with an
epilogue.   "An epilogue, my dear sir," cried
Sheridan ; " it will never come to that ! "

In talking over the true theory of the Preface
with friends engaged in other trades than that of
letters, I have found that the same principle obtains elsewhere. A learned professor told me that
he never declared the limitations of his course in
his first lecture ; he preferred to begin by getting
the attention of the students ; when he had once
acquired this, why, then he found occasion casu-

ally in the second or third, or even the fourth
lecture, to let his hearers know, as if by accident,
just what bounds he proposed to set to his dis-
course.   The case of the dramatist is even harder,
for an acknowledgment of any kind printed in the
playbill, before the curtain rises on the first act for
the first time, is more dangerous than the most
apologetic Preface.   Dramatists have always
availed themselves of the royal privilege of prig-
ging — or, if this sound unseemly, let us say, of
taking their goods wherever they found them.   So
many playwrights have presented as new and
original plays which were neither new nor original,
that critics are wary and suspicious.   They are
inclined to believe the worst of their fellow-man
when he has written a play : after all, as M. Thiers
said, it is so easy not to write a tragedy in five
acts.   But if a man has written a tragedy in five
acts or a comedy in three, if a man is an honest
man, and if he is under some trifling obligations
to some forgotten predecessor, what is he to do?
The critics are sure to suppose that the author has
understated his indebtedness.   If he say he took a
hint for a scene or a character from Schiller or Sir
Walter Scott or Alexandre Dumas, the critics are
likely to record that the play is derived from
Schiller, or Scott, or Dumas.   If he say his plot

was suggested by a part of an old play, they are
likely to set it down as founded on the old play.
If he confess that his piece is remotely based on
another in a foreign tongue, they call it an adaptation. And if he, in the excess of his honesty, pre-
sents his play humbly as an adaptation, they go a
step farther and accept it as a translation, and are
even capable of finding fault with it because it
does not exactly reproduce the original.   If Mr.
Pinero, when in his charming comedy, the
' Squire,' he sought to bring the scent of the hay
across the footlights, had made an allusion to Mr.
Hardy's story, not a few dramatic critics would
have called the play an adaptation of the story —
which it was not.   It is impossible for the dramatist to frame an acknowledgment which shall
declare with mathematical precision his indebtedness to any given predecessor for a bit of color,
for a vague suggestion of character, for a stray hint
of a situation, or for a small but pregnant knot of
man and motive.   It cannot be set down in plain
figures.   Unfortunately for him who writes for
the stage, the playbill which everybody reads
is the only Preface ; and there are no foot-notes
possible. The dramatist has to confess his obligation at the very worst moment, or else forever
after hold his peace.

"A Preface, being the entrance to a book, should invite by its beauty. An elegant porch announces the splendor of the interior," said the elder Disraeli, setting forth the theory of the Preface as it was in the past. But this is not the new and true theory of the Preface, which should be written in letters of gold in the study of every maker of books :— "If you want to have your book criticized favorably, give yourself a good notice in the Preface ! " This is the true theory, in the very words of its discoverer. If it is not absolutely sound and water-tight, it is, at all events, an admirable working hypothesis. Although others had had faint glimmerings of the truth, it was left for a friend of mine to formulate it finally and as I have given it here. To him are due the thanks of all makers of books — and he is a publisher.

THE PHILOSOPHY OF THE SHORT-STORY.

F it chance that artists fall to talking about their art, it is the critic's place to listen, that he may pick up a little knowledge. Of late, certain of the novelists of Great Britain and the United States have been discussing the principles and the practice of the art of writing stories. Mr. Howells declared his warm appreciation of Mr. Henry James's novels ; Mr. Stevenson made public a delightful plea for Romance ; Mr. Besant lectured gracefully on the Art of Fiction ; and Mr. James modestly presented his views by way of supplement and criticism. The discussion took a wide range. With more or less fulness it covered the proper aim and intent of the novelist, his material and his methods, his success, his rewards, social and pecuniary, and the morality of his work and of his art. But, with all its extension, the discussion did not include one important branch of the art of fiction : it did not consider at all the minor art of the Short-story. Although neither Mr.

Howells nor Mr. James, Mr. Besant nor Mr. Stevenson specifically limited his remarks to those longer, and, in the picture dealer's sense of the word, more "important," tales known as Novels, and, although, of course, their general criticisms of the abstract principles of the art of fiction applied quite as well to the Short-story as to the Novel, yet all their concrete examples were full-length Novels, and the Short-story, as such, received no recognition at all.

The difference between a Novel and a Novelette is one of length only : a Novelette is a brief Novel. But the difference between a Novel and a Short-story is a difference of kind. A true Short-story is something other and something more than a mere story which is short. A true Short-story differs from the Novel chiefly in its essential unity of impression. In a far more exact and precise use of the word, a Short-story has unity as a Novel cannot have it. Often, it may be noted by the way, the Short-story fulfils the three false unities of the French classic drama : it shows one action in one place on one day. A Short-story deals with a single character, a single event, a single emotion, or the series of emotions called forth by a single situation. Poe's paradox that a poem cannot greatly exceed a hundred lines in length under penalty of ceasing to be one poem and breaking into a string of poems, may serve to suggest the precise difference between the Short-story and the Novel. The Short-story is the single effect, complete and self-contained, while the Novel is of necessity broken into a series of episodes. Thus the Short-story has, what the Novel cannot have, the effect of "totality," as Poe called it, the unity of impression. The Short-story is not only not a chapter out of a Novel, or an incident or an episode extracted from a longer tale, but at its best it impresses the reader with the belief that it would be spoiled if it were made larger or if it were incorporated into a more elaborate work. The difference in spirit and in form between the Lyric and the Epic is scarcely greater than the difference between the Short-story and the Novel; and the 'Raven' and 'How we brought the good news from Ghent to Aix' are not more unlike the 'Lady of the Lake' and 'Paradise Lost,' in form and in spirit, than the 'Luck of Roaring Camp' and the 'Man without a Country,' two typical Short-stories, are unlike 'Vanity Fair' and the 'Heart of Midlothian,' two typical Novels.

Another great difference between the Short-story and the Novel lies in the fact that the Novel, nowadays at least, must be a love-tale, while the

Short-story need not deal with love at all. Although 'Vanity Fair' was a Novel without a Hero, nearly every other Novel has a hero and a heroine, and the novelist, however unwillingly, must concern himself in their love-affairs. But the writer of Short-stories is under no bonds of this sort. Of course he may tell a tale of love if he choose, and if love enters into his tale naturally and to its enriching; but he need not bother with love at all unless he please. Some of the best of Short-stories are love-stories too,—Mr. Aldrich's 'Marjory Daw' for instance, Mr. Stimson's 'Mrs. Knollys,' Mr. Bunner's 'Love in Old Cloathes'; but more of them are not love-stories at all. If we were to pick out the ten best Short-stories, I think we should find that fewer than half of them made any mention at all of love. In the 'Snow Image' and in the 'Ambitious Guest,' in the 'Gold Bug' and in the 'Fall of the House of Usher,' in 'My Double, and how he Undid me,' in 'Devil-Puzzlers,' in the 'Outcasts of Poker Flat,' in 'Jean-ah Poquelin,' in 'A Bundle of Letters,' there is little or no mention of the love of man for woman, which is the chief topic of conversation in a Novel. While the Novel cannot get on without love, the Short-story can. Since love is almost the only thing which will give interest to a long story, the writer of

Novels has to get love into his tales as best he may, even when the subject rebels and when he himself is too old to take any interest in the mating of John and Joan. But the Short-story, being brief, does not need a love-interest to hold its parts together, and the writer of Short-stories has thus a greater freedom: he may do as he pleases ; from him a love-tale is not expected.

But other things are required of a writer of Short-stories which are not required of a writer of Novels. The novelist may take his time : he has abundant room to turn about. The writer of Short-stories must be concise, and compression, a vigorous compression, is essential. For him, more than for any one else, the half is more than the whole. Again, the novelist may be common-place, he may bend his best energies to the photographic reproduction of the actual; if he show us a cross section of real life we are content ; but the writer of Short-stories must have originality and ingenuity. If to compression, originality, and ingenuity he add also a touch of fantasy, so much the better. It may be said that no one has ever succeeded as a writer of Short-stories who had not ingenuity, originality, and compression, and that most of those who have succeeded in this line had also the touch of fantasy. But there are not a few successful novelists lacking not only in fantasy and compression, but also in ingenuity and originality: they had other qualities, no doubt, but these they had not. If an example must be given, the name of Anthony Trollope will occur to all. Fantasy was a thing he abhorred; compression he knew not; and originality and ingenuity can be conceded to him only by a strong stretch of the ordinary meaning of the words. Other qualities he had in plenty, but not these. And, not having them, he was not a writer of Short-stories. Judging from his essay on Hawthorne, one may even go so far as to say that Trollope did not know a good Short-story when he saw it.

I have written Short-story with a capital S and a hyphen because I wished to emphasize the distinction between the Short-story and the story which is merely short. The Short-story is a high and difficult department of fiction. The story which is short can be written by anybody who can write at all; and it may be good, bad, or indifferent; but at its best it is wholly unlike the Short-story. In 'An Editor's Tales' Trollope has given us excellent specimens of the story which is short; and the stories which make up this book are amusing enough and clever enough, but they are wanting in the individuality and in the completeness of the genuine Short-story. Like the brief tales to be seen in the English monthly magazines and in the Sunday editions of American newspapers into which they are copied, they are, for the most part, either merely amplified anecdotes or else incidents which might have been used in a Novel just as well as not. Now, the genuine Short-story abhors the idea of the Novel. It can be conceived neither as part of a Novel nor as elaborated and expanded so as to form a Novel. A good Short-story is no more the synopsis of a Novel than it is an episode from a Novel. A slight Novel, or a Novel cut down, is a Novelette: it is not a Short-story. Mr. Howells's ' Their Wedding Journey' and Miss Howard's ' One Summer' are Novelettes,—little Novels. Mr. Anstey's ' Vice Versa,' Mr. Besant's ' Case of Mr. Lucraft,' Hugh Conway's ' Called Back,' Mr. Julian Hawthorne's 'Archibald Malmaison,' and Mr. Stevenson's ' Strange Case of Dr. Jekyll and Mr. Hyde' are Short-stories in conception, although they are without the compression which the Short-story requires. In the acute and learned essay on *vers de société* which Mr. Frederick Locker prefixed to his admirable ' Lyra Elegantiarum,' he declared that the two characteristics of the best *vers de*

4

société were brevity and brilliancy, and that the
'Rape of the Lock' would be the type and model
of the best *vers de société*—if it were not just a
little too long. So it is with the 'Case of Mr.
Lucraft,' with 'Vice Versa,' with 'Archibald Malmaison': they are just a little too long.

It is to be noted as a curious coincidence that
there is no exact word in English to designate
either *vers de société* or the Short-story, and yet in
no language are there better *vers de société* or
Short-stories than in English. It may be remarked also that there is a certain likeness between *vers de société* and Short-stories : for one
thing, both seem easy to write and are hard.
And the typical qualifications of each may apply
with almost equal force to the other : *vers de
société* should reveal compression, ingenuity, and
originality, and Short-stories should have brevity
and brilliancy. In no class of writing are neatness
of construction and polish of execution more
needed than in the writing of *vers de société* and
of Short-stories. The writer of Short-stories
must have the sense of form, which Mr. Lathrop
has called "the highest and last attribute of a
creative writer." The construction must be logical, adequate, harmonious. Here is the weak
spot in Mr. Bishop's 'One of the Thirty Pieces,'

the fundamental idea of which has extraordinary
strength perhaps not fully developed in the story.
But other of Mr. Bishop's stories — the ' Battle of
Bunkerloo,' for instance — are admirable in all
ways, conception and execution having an even
excellence.   Again, Hugh Conway's ' Daughter
of the Stars ' is a Short-story which fails from
sheer deficiency of style : here is one of the very
finest Short-story ideas ever given to mortal man,
but the handling is at best barely sufficient.   To
do justice to the conception would task the execution of a poet.   We can merely wonder what the
tale would have been had it occurred to Hawthorne, to Poe, or to Théophile Gautier.   An idea
logically developed by one possessing the sense of
form and the gift of style is what we look for in
the Short-story.

But, although the sense of form and the gift of
style are essential to the writing of a good Short-
story, they are secondary to the idea, to the conception, to the subject.   Those who hold, with a
certain American novelist, that it is no matter what
you have to say, but only how you say it, need not
attempt the Short-story; for the Short-story, far
more than the Novel even, demands a subject.
The Short-story is nothing if there is no story to
tell.   The Novel, so Mr. James told us not long

ago, "is, in its broadest definition, a personal impression of life." The most powerful force in French fiction to-day is M. Emile Zola, chiefly known in America and England, I fear me greatly, by the dirt which masks and degrades the real beauty and firm strength not seldom concealed in his novels; and M. Emile Zola declares that the novelist of the future will not concern himself with the artistic evolution of a plot: he will take *une histoire quelconque*, any kind of a story, and make it serve his purpose,—which is to give elaborate pictures of life in all its most minute details. The acceptance of these theories is a negation of the Short-story. Important as are form and style, the subject of the Short-story is of more importance yet. What you have to tell is of greater interest than how you tell it. I once heard a clever American novelist pour sarcastic praise upon another American novelist,—for novelists, even American novelists, do not always dwell together in unity. The subject of the eulogy is the chief of those who have come to be known as the International Novelists, and he was praised because he had invented and made possible a fifth plot. Hitherto, declared the eulogist, only four terminations of a novel have been known to the most enthusiastic and untiring student of fiction.

First, they are married; or, second, she marries
some one else; or, thirdly, he marries some one
else; or, fourthly, and lastly, she dies. Now,
continued the panegyrist, a fifth termination
has been shown to be practicable : they are not
married, she does not die, he does not die, and
nóthing happens at all. As a Short-story need
not be a love-story, it is of no consequence at all
whether they marry or die; but a Short-story in
which nothing happens at all is an absolute im-
possibility.

Perhaps the difference between a Short-story
and a Sketch can best be indicated by saying that,
while a Sketch may be still-life, in a Short-story
something always happens. A Sketch may be an
outline of character, or even a picture of a mood
of mind, but in a Short-story there must be something done, there must be an action. Yet the
distinction, like that between the Novel and the
Romance, is no longer of vital importance. In the
preface to the ' House of the Seven Gables,' Hawthorne sets forth the difference between the Novel
and the Romance, and claims for himself the privileges of the romancer. Mr. Henry James fails to
see this difference. The fact is, that the Short-
story and the Sketch, the Novel and the Romance,
melt and merge one into the other, and no man

may mete the boundaries of each, though their extremes lie far apart. With the more complete understanding of the principle of development and evolution in literary art, as in physical nature, we see the futility of a strict and rigid classification into precisely defined genera and species. All that is needful for us to remark now is that the Short-story has limitless possibilities : it may be as realistic as the most prosaic novel, or as fantastic as the most ethereal romance.

As a touch of fantasy, however slight, is a welcome ingredient in a Short-story, and as the American takes more thought of things unseen than the Englishman, we may have here an incomplete explanation of the superiority of the American Short-story over the English. "John Bull has suffered the idea of the Invisible to be very much fattened out of him," says Mr. Lowell: "Jonathan is conscious still that he lives in the World of the Unseen as well as of the Seen." It is not enough to catch a ghost white-handed and to hale him into the full glare of the electric light. A brutal misuse of the supernatural is perhaps the very lowest degradation of the art of fiction. But "to mingle the marvellous rather as a slight, delicate, and evanescent flavor than as any actual portion of the substance," to quote from the preface to

the 'House of the Seven Gables,' this is, or should
be, the aim of the writer of Short-stories whenever his feet leave the firm ground of fact as he
strays in the unsubstantial realms of fantasy.   In
no one's writings is this better exemplified than
in Hawthorne's; not even in Poe's.   There is a
propriety in Hawthorne's fantasy to which Poe
could not attain.   Hawthorne's effects are moral
where Poe's are merely physical.   The situation
and its logical development and the effects to be
got out of it are all Poe thinks of.   In Hawthorne
the situation, however strange and weird, is
only the outward and visible sign of an inward
and spiritual struggle.   Ethical consequences are
always worrying Hawthorne's soul: but Poe did
not know that there were any ethics.

There are literary evolutionists who, in their
whim of seeing in every original writer a copy of
some predecessor, have declared that Hawthorne
is derived from Tieck, and Poe from Hoffmann,
just as Dickens modelled himself on Smollett and
Thackeray followed in the footsteps of Fielding.
In all four cases the pupil surpassed the master,—if haply Tieck and Hoffmann can be considered as even remotely the masters of Hawthorne
and Poe.   When Coleridge was told that Klopstock
was the German Milton, he assented with the dry

addendum, "A very German Milton." So is
Hoffmann a very German Poe, and Tieck a very
German Hawthorne. Of a truth, both Poe and
Hawthorne are as American as any one can be. If
the adjective American has any meaning at all, it
qualifies Poe and Hawthorne. They were American to the core. They both revealed the curious
sympathy with Oriental moods of thought which
is often an American characteristic. Poe, with his
cold logic and his mathematical analysis, and Hawthorne, with his introspective conscience and his
love of the subtile and the invisible, are repre-
sentative of phases of American character not to
be mistaken by any one who has given thought
to the influence of nationality.

As to which of the two was the greater, discussion is idle, but that Hawthorne was the finer
genius few would deny. Poe, as cunning an
artificer of goldsmith's work, and as adroit in its
vending as was ever M. Josse, declared that
"Hawthorne's distinctive trait is invention, creation, imagination, originality,—a trait which in
the literature of fiction is positively worth all the
rest." But with the moral basis of Hawthorne's
work, which had flowered in the crevices and
crannies of New England Puritanism, Poe did not
concern himself. In Poe's hands the story of the

'Ambitious Guest' might have thrilled us with a
more powerful horror, but it would have lacked
the ethical beauty which Hawthorne gave it and
which makes it significant beyond a mere feat of
verbal legerdemain. And the subtile simplicity of
the 'Great Stone Face' is as far from Poe as the
pathetic irony of the 'Ambitious Guest.' In all
his most daring fantasies Hawthorne is natural,
and, though he may project his vision far beyond
the boundaries of fact, nowhere does he violate
the laws of nature. He had at all times a wholesome simplicity, and he never showed any trace
of the morbid taint which characterizes nearly all
Poe's work. Hawthorne, one may venture to
say, had the broad sanity of genius, while we
should understand any one who might declare
that Poe had mental disease raised to the nth.

Although it may be doubted whether the fiery
and tumultuous rush of a volcano, which may be
taken to typify Poe, is as powerful or impressive
in the end as the calm and inevitable progression
of a glacier, to which, for the purposes of this
comparison only, we may liken Hawthorne, yet
the effect and influence of Poe's work are indisputable. One might hazard the assertion that in
all Latin countries he is the best known of American authors. Certainly no American writer has

4*

been as widely accepted in France. Nothing better of its kind has ever been done than the 'Pit
and the Pendulum,' or than the 'Fall of the House
of Usher,' which Mr. Stoddard has compared recently with Browning's 'Childe Roland to the
Dark Tower came' for its power of suggesting
intellectual desolation. Nothing better of its kind
has ever been done than the 'Gold Bug,' or than
the 'Purloined Letter,' or than the 'Murders in
the Rue Morgue.' This last, indeed, is a story of
marvellous skill : it was the first of its kind, and
to this day it remains a model, not only unsur-
passed, but unapproachable. It was the first of
detective stories; and it has had thousands of imi-
tations and no rival. The originality, the ingenuity, the verisimilitude of this tale and of its fellows
are beyond all praise. Poe had a faculty which
one may call imaginative ratiocination to a degree
beyond all other writers of fiction. He did not at
all times keep up to the high level, in one style,
of the 'Fall of the House of Usher,' and in another
of the 'Murders in the Rue Morgue,' and it was
not to be expected that he should. Only too
often did he sink to the grade of the ordinary
'Tale from *Blackwood*,' which he himself satir-
ized in his usual savage vein of humor. Yet even
in his flimsiest and most tawdry tales we see the

truth of Mr. Lowell's assertion that Poe had "two of the prime qualities of genius,—a faculty of vigorous yet minute analysis, and a wonderful fecundity of imagination." Mr. Lowell said also that Poe combined "in a very remarkable manner two faculties which are seldom found united,—a power of influencing the mind of the reader by the impalpable shadows of mystery and a minuteness of detail which does not leave a pin or a button unnoticed. Both are, in truth, the natural results of the predominating quality of his mind, to which we have before alluded,—analysis." In Poe's hands, however, the enumeration of pins and buttons, the exact imitation of the prosaic facts of humdrum life in this workaday world, is not an end, but a means only, whereby he constructs and intensifies the shadow of mystery which broods over the things thus realistically portrayed.

With the recollection that it is more than half a century since Hawthorne and Poe wrote their best Short-stories, it is not a little comic to see now and again in American newspapers a rash assertion that "American literature has hitherto been deficient in good Short-stories," or the reckless declaration that "the art of writing Short-stories has not hitherto been cultivated in the United

States." Nothing could be more inexact than these statements. Almost as soon as America began to have any literature at all it had good Short-stories. It is quite within ten, or at the most twenty, years that the American novel has come to the front and forced the acknowledgment of its equality with the English novel and the French novel; but for fifty years the American Short-story has had a supremacy which any competent critic could not but acknowledge. Indeed, the present excellence of the American novel is due in great measure to the Short-story; for nearly every one of the American novelists whose works are now read by the whole English-speaking race began as a writer of Short-stories. Although as a form of fiction the Short-story is not inferior to the Novel, and although it is not easier, all things considered, yet its brevity makes its composition simpler for the 'prentice hand. Though the Short-stories of the beginner may not be good, yet in the writing of Short-stories he shall learn how to tell a story, he shall discover by experience the elements of the art of fiction more readily and, above all, more quickly than if he had begun on a long and exhausting novel. The physical strain of writing a full-sized novel is far greater than the reader can well imagine. To this strain the beginner in fiction may gradually accustom himself by the composition of Short-stories.

(Here, if the digression may be pardoned, occasion serves to say that if our writers of plays had the same chance that our writers of novels have, we might now have a school of American dramatists of which we should be as proud as of our school of American novelists. In dramatic composition, the equivalent of the Short-story is the one-act play, be it drama or comedy or comedietta or farce. As the novelists have learned their trade by the writing of Short-stories, so the dramatists might learn their trade, far more difficult as it is and more complicated, by the writing of one-act plays. But, while the magazines of the United States are hungry for good Short-stories, and sift carefully all that are sent to them, in the hope of happening on a treasure, the theatres of the United States are closed to one-act plays, and the dramatist is denied the opportunity of making a humble and tentative beginning. The conditions of the theatre are such that there is little hope of a change for the better in this respect,—more's the pity. The manager has a tradition that a "broken bill," a programme containing more than one play, is a confession of weakness, and he prefers, so far as possible, to keep his weakness concealed.)

When we read the roll of American novelists, we see that nearly all of them began as writers of Short-stories.   Some of them, Mr. Bret Harte, for instance, and Mr. Edward Everett Hale, never got any farther, or, at least, if they wrote novels, their novels did not receive the full artistic appreciation and popular approval bestowed on their Short-stories.   Even Mr. Cable's ' Grandissimes' has not made his readers forget his ' Posson Jone,' nor has Mr. Aldrich's ' Queen of Sheba,' charming as she was, driven from our memory his ' Marjory Daw,' as delightful and as captivating as that other non-existent heroine, Mr. Austin Dobson's ' Dorothy.'   Mrs. Burnett, Miss Woolson, and Miss Murfree put forth volumes of Short-stories before they attempted the more sustained flight of the full-fledged Novel.   Miss Jewett, Mr. Bunner, Mr. Bishop, and Mr. Julian Hawthorne wrote Short-stories before they wrote novels ; and Mr. James has never gathered into a book from the back-numbers of magazines the half of his earlier efforts.

In these references to the American magazine I believe I have suggested the real reason of the superiority of the American Short-stories over the English.   It is not only that the eye of patriotism may detect more fantasy, more humor, a finer feeling for art, in these younger United States, but there is a more emphatic and material reason for the American proficiency. There is in the United States a demand for Short-stories which does not exist in Great Britain, or at any rate not in the same degree. The Short-story is of very great importance to the American magazine. But in the British magazine the serial Novel is the one thing of consequence, and all else is termed ''padding.'' In England the writer of three-volume Novels is the best paid of literary laborers. So in England whoever has the gift of story-telling is strongly tempted not to essay the difficult art of writing Short-stories, for which he will receive only an inadequate reward ; and he is as strongly tempted to write a long story which may serve first as a serial and afterward as a three-volume Novel. The result of this temptation is seen in the fact that there is not a single English novelist whose reputation has been materially assisted by the Short-stories he has written. More than once in the United States a single Short-story has made a man known, but in Great Britain such an event is well-nigh impossible. The disastrous effect on narrative art of the desire to distend every subject to the three-volume limit has been dwelt on unceasingly by English critics.

The three-volume system is peculiar to Great Britain : it does not obtain either in France or the United States. As a consequence, the French and American writer of fiction is left free to treat his subject at the length it demands,—no more and no less. It is pleasant to note that there are signs of the beginning of the break-up of the system even in England ; and the protests of the chief English critics against it are loud and frequent. It is responsible in great measure for the invention and protection of the British machine for making English Novels, of which Mr. Warner told us in his entertaining essay on fiction. We all know the work of this machine, and we all recognize the trade-mark it imprints in the corner. But Mr. Warner failed to tell us, what nevertheless is a fact, that this British machine can be geared down so as to turn out the English short story. Now, the English short story, as the machine makes it and as we see it in most English magazines, is only a little English Novel, or an incident or episode from an English Novel. It is thus the exact artistic opposite of the American Short-story, of which, as we have seen, the chief characteristics are originality, ingenuity, compression, and, not infrequently, a touch of fantasy. I do not say, of course, that the good and genuine Short-story is not written in England now and then,—for if I were to make any such assertion some of the best work of Mr. Stevenson, of Mr. Besant, and of Mr. Anstey would rise up to contradict me ; but this is merely an accidental growth, and not a staple of production. As a rule, in England the artist in fiction does not care to hide his light under a bushel, and he puts his best work where it will be seen of all men,—that is to say, *not* in a Short-story. So it happens that the most of the brief tales in the English magazines are not true Short-stories at all, and that they belong to a lower form of the art of fiction, in the department with the amplified anecdote. It is the three-volume Novel which has killed the Short-story in England.

Certain of the remarks in the present paper I put forth first anonymously in the columns of the *Saturday Review*. To my intense surprise, they were controverted in the *Nation*. The critic began by assuming that the writer had said that Americans preferred Short-stories to Novels. What had really been said was that there was a steady demand for Short-stories in American magazines, whereas in England the demand was rather for serial Novels. "In the first place," said the critic, "Americans do not prefer Short-stories, as is shown by the enormous number of British

Novels circulated among us; and in the second place, tales of the quiet, domestic kind, which form the staple of periodicals like *All the Year Round* and *Chambers's Journal*, have here thousands of readers where native productions, however clever and original, have only hundreds, since the former are reprinted by the country papers and in the Sunday editions of city papers as rapidly and regularly as they are produced at home." Now, the answer to this is simply that these English Novels and English stories are reprinted widely in the United States, not because the American people prefer them to anything else, but because, owing to the absence of international copyright, they cost nothing. That the American people prefer to read American stories when they can get them is shown by the enormous circulation of the periodicals which make a specialty of American fiction.

I find I have left myself little space to speak of the Short-story as it exists in other literatures than those of Great Britain and the United States. The conditions which have killed the Short-story in England do not obtain elsewhere; and elsewhere there are not a few good writers of Short-stories. Turgenef, Björnsen, Sacher-Masoch, Freytag, Lindau, are the names which one recalls

at once and without effort as masters in the
art and mystery of the Short-story. Turgenef's
Short-stories, in particular, it would be difficult to
commend too warmly. But it is in France that
the Short-story flourishes most abundantly. In
France the conditions are not unlike those in the
United States ; and, although there are few French
magazines, there are many Parisian newspapers
of a wide hospitality to literature. The demand
for the Short-story has called forth an abundant
supply. Among the writers of the last generation
who excelled in the *conte* — which is almost the
exact French equivalent for Short-story, as *nou-
velle* may be taken to indicate the story which is
merely short, the episode, the incident, the amplified anecdote — were Alfred de Musset, Théophile
Gautier, and Prosper Mérimée. The best work
of Mérimée has never been surpassed. As compression was with him almost a mania, as, indeed,
it was with his friend Turgenef, he seemed born on
purpose to write Short-stories. Turgenef carried
his desire for conciseness so far that he seems always to be experimenting to see how much of his
story he may leave out. One of the foremost writers of *contes* is Edmond About, whose exquisite
humor is known to all readers of the ' Man with
the Broken Ear,' — a Short-story in conception,

though unduly extended in execution. Few of the charming *contes* of M. Alphonse Daudet, or of the earlier Short-stories of M. Emile Zola, have been translated into English ; and the poetic tales of M. François Coppée are likewise unduly neglected in this country. The ʻ Abbé Constantin ʼ of M. Ludovic Halévy has been read by many, but the Gallic satire of his more Parisian Short-stories has been neglected, perhaps wisely, in spite of their broad humor and their sharp wit. In the *contes* of M. Guy de Maupassant there is a manly vigor pushed at times to excess; and in the very singular collection of stories which M. Jean Richepin has called the ʻ Morts Bizarres ʼ we find a modern continuation of the Poe tradition, always more potent in France than elsewhere. I have given this list of French writers of Short-stories merely as evidence that the art flourishes in France as well as in the United States, and not at all with a view of recommending the fair readers of this essaylet to send at once for the works of these French writers, which are not always—indeed, one may say not often—in exact accordance with the conventionalities of Anglo-Saxon propriety.

The Short-story should not be void or without form, but its form may be whatever the author please. He has an absolute liberty of choice. It may be a personal narrative, like Poe's 'Descent into the Maelstrom' or Mr. Hale's 'My Double, and how he Undid me'; it may be impersonal, like Mr. Perkins's 'Devil-Puzzlers' or Colonel De Forest's 'Brigade Commander'; it may be a conundrum, like Mr. Stockton's insoluble query, the 'Lady or the Tiger?' it may be 'A Bundle of Letters,' like Mr. James's story, or 'A Letter and a Paragraph,' like Mr. Bunner's; it may be a medley of letters and telegrams and narrative, like Mr. Aldrich's 'Marjory Daw'; it may be cast in any one of these forms, or in a combination of all of them, or in a wholly new form, if haply such may yet be found by diligent search. Whatever its form, it should have symmetry of design. If it have also wit or humor, pathos or poetry, and especially a distinct and unmistakable flavor of originality, so much the better. But the chief requisites are compression, originality, ingenuity, and now and again a touch of fantasy. Sometimes we may detect in a writer of Short-stories a tendency toward the over-elaboration of ingenuity, toward the exhibition of ingenuity for its own sake, as in a Chinese puzzle. But mere cleverness is incompatible with greatness, and to commend a writer as "very clever" is not to give him high praise. From this fault of super-

subtilty women are free for the most part.   They
are more likely than men to rely on broad human
emotion, and their tendency in error is toward the
morbid analysis of a high-strung moral situation.

TWO LATTER-DAY LYRISTS.

I.

MR. FREDERICK LOCKER.

ATRICIAN rhymes" is the apt phrase Mr. Stedman coined to characterize that kind of *vers de société*, nameless in English, which is more than mere society-verse. It describes Mr. Locker's poetry more accurately than Mr. Austin Dobson's, for example, or Mr. Calverley's, since Mr. Locker confines himself more strictly within the circle of "good society," of Park Lane, and of fashion. Mr. Locker is the du Maurier of song, and his 'London Lyrics' are as entertaining and as instructive to the student of Victorian manners as Mr. du Maurier's 'Pictures of English Society.' Mr. Locker has succeeded Praed as the laureate of the world, and he ignores the flesh, and is ignorant of the devil, just like Praed, and just like society itself. But it seems to me that Mr. Locker's range is wider than Praed's, whose success lay

almost altogether in his songs of society; Praed
was out of place when he ventured far from May-
fair and beyond the sound of St. George's in Han-
over Square; while Mr. Locker's Pegasus pauses
at the mouth of Cité Fadette as gracefully as it
treads the gravel of Rotten Row. The later poet
has wider sympathies than the elder, who, indeed,
may be said to have had but one note. The
'Vicar' is a beautiful bit of verse, but its touch of
tenderness sets it apart from all Praed's other
work, which is brilliant with a hard and metallic
brilliancy. Praed dazzles almost to weariness;
his lines stand out sharply like fireworks at midnight. More brilliant than Praed no poet could
well be. More pleasing Mr. Locker is, and he
gives a higher pleasure. He has wit like Praed,
but far more humor; and the soft radiance of
humor never tires the eye like the quick flashes of
wit. With broader humor, he has a broader
humanity and a finer individuality. In short, the
difference between the two may be summed up
in favor of the younger man, by saying that Mr.
Locker can write Praedesque poems,—compare
the 'Belle of the Ball-room,' for instance, and
'A *Nice* Correspondent,'— while it may well be
doubted whether Praed could have emulated Mr.
Locker's 'To My Mistress' and 'At Her Window.'

Of course, it is easy to say that Mr. Locker continues the tradition of Prior and Praed; it is easy also to see that, in two respects, at least, the progression shows the progress of the age. One improvement is in the form used by the poet; the other in the feeling, the temper of the poet himself. Praed contented himself with putting his best work into the eight-line stanza, now a little worn from overwork:

> Our love was like most other loves;
>   A little glow, a little shiver,
> A rosebud and a pair of gloves,
>   And 'Fly not yet'—upon the river;
> Some jealousy of some one's heir,
>   Some hopes of dying broken-hearted,
> A miniature, a lock of hair,
>   The usual vows—and then we parted.

In this metre, Mr. Locker and Mr. Austin Dobson, in England, and Mr. Saxe, in America, have written verses that Praed might not disown; but though the metal was theirs, the mould was Praed's. Mr. Locker's best work has not gone into any one form; he has wisely varied his metre; he has invented of his own, and he has borrowed from his neighbor. 'A *Nice* Correspondent' is Swinburnian in its rhythm, and

5

'To My Grandmother' repeats the measures of
Holmes's 'Last Leaf,' a delightful and most difficult metre, lending itself easily to intricate har-
monies, and not to be attempted now by meaner
hands :

> This Relative of mine,
> Was she seventy-and-nine
>   When she died?
> By the canvas may be seen
> How she looked at seventeen,
>   As a Bride.

> Beneath a summer tree
> Her maiden reverie
>   Has a charm :
> Her ringlets are in taste ;
> What an arm ! . . . what a waist
>   For an arm !

Is not this the perfection of daintiness and delicacy? Is it not delightful—this mingling of sly
fun and playful banter? And this brings us to
the second quality, in which Mr. Locker and Mr.
Dobson are plainly superior to Prior and Praed—
in their treatment of woman. Prior thought of
women with little feeling, and he wrote of them
with little respect ; however much he might pretend to worship a dame or a damsel, he kept a

keen and unkind eye on her failings. At all times
his tone toward women is one of good-natured
contempt, often ill-concealed. With Praed, a
complete change had come in the attitude ; he
is avowedly a friendly critic, and yet his verse
catches no tinge of warmth from his friendliness.
Though he may have felt deeply, he lets his scepticism and his wit hide his feeling until we are
well-nigh forced to doubt whether he had any
feeling to hide. The lively beauties who figure in
Praed's glittering verse are far more true to life
than the French fictions of Prior, but the ladies of
Mr. Locker and Mr. Dobson are quite as charming and indubitably more natural. They are true
women, too, not mere figments of the fancy ;
they are the result of later and deeper observation ;
and they have far more variety from the given
prototype. Prior wrote of women at large, and
Praed rang the changes on the ' Belle of the Ball-
room.' Now, Mr. Locker has a gallery of girls, all
fresh and ingenuous young maidens. Prior did
not respect women ; Praed admired them coldly ;
Mr. Locker has a warm regard for them and a
manly respect, and also a demure humor which
sees into their wiles and their weaknesses quite as
sharply as did Prior or Praed.

Having set forth thus some of the things which

Mr. Locker, the poet, is and is not, it may be well
to give a few facts about Mr. Locker, the man.   He
was born in 1821.   His father, Edward Hawke
Locker, was in the public service, and took a
warm interest in literature and art.   His grandfather, Captain W. Locker, R. N., was an old
friend of Lord Nelson's ; and both Collingwood
and Nelson served under him.   Mr. Locker composed little until late in life, or at least until he was
thirty ; and he found great difficulty, so he wrote
to a friend, " in persuading editors to have anything to say to my verses ; but Thackeray believed
in me, and used to say, ' Never mind, Locker, our
verse *may* be small beer, but at any rate it is the
right tap.' "   Thus encouraged, Mr. Locker wrote
on, and in time editors began to relent.   In 1857
he gathered his scattered poems and put them forth
in a single volume as 'London Lyrics.'   As edition
followed edition he has added the few poems he
has written of laté years, and has dropped those of
his earlier poems that he thought unworthy.   The
latest published edition—the eighth, I think it
is—is scarcely any heavier than the first.   Later
than this, however, is a little book, beautifully
printed and beautifully bound, which Mr. Locker
has recently given to his friends, and which contains a special selection of his very best work,

made by Mr. Austin Dobson, who has prefixed
this friendly little sextain :

> Apollo made, one April day,
> A new thing in the rhyming way;
> Its turn was neat, its wit was clear,
> It wavered 'twixt a smile and tear;
> Then Momus gave a touch satiric,
> And it became a 'London Lyric.'

Besides putting his own *vers de société* into a
book, Mr. Locker made a collection, under the title
of 'Lyra Elegantiarum,' of the best specimens in
English of the *vers de société* and *vers d'occasion* of
poets no longer living.   Of this a new and revised
edition was published in 1867 ; it is a model of what
such a selection should be ; and it was ushered in by
an essay of the editor's—all too brief—on the art
of writing *vers de société*.   In 1879 Mr. Locker published a most amusing little volume of 'Patch-
work,' containing bits of rhyme and bits of talk,
with here a jest and there a joke, excerpts from
his commonplace book, and enlivened with a few
of the anecdotes he is wont to tell most effectively.
For the lyrist of London is no recluse ; he is a man
of the world, even more than he is a man of letters.
In life as in literature he has both humor and good-
humor.   Although satiric by nature, he is thor-

oughly sympathetic and generous.   Well-to-do in
the world, he has been able to indulge his liking
for the little things in art which make life worth
living.   His collections of china, of drawings, of
engravings, are all excellent; and his literary
curiosities, first editions of great books and
precious autographs of great men, make a poor
American wickedly envious.   He is a connoisseur
of the best type, never buying trash or bargain-
hunting; knowing what he wants, and why he
wants it, and what it is worth; and his treasures
are freely opened to any literary brother who is
seeking after truth.

In studying Mr. Locker's pictures of English
society we cannot but feel that the poet has drawn
his lines with the living model before him.   It is in
the distinctively London-town lyrics—in the ' Pil-
grims of Pall Mall,' in 'Rotten Row,' in 'At Hurl-
ingham,' in 'St. James' Street,' and in 'Piccadilly,'—

> Piccadilly!   Shops, palaces, bustle, and breeze,
>   The whirring of wheels and the murmur of trees,
> By night or by day, whether noisy or stilly,
>   Whatever my mood is, I love Piccadilly.

—it is in these that Mr. Locker most shows the
influence of Praed, which is decidedly less apparent
in the less local poems,—in ' A Garden Lyric,' in

'On an Old Muff,' in 'Geraldine,' and in the sportive
and brightsome lines on 'A Human Skull':

> A human Skull, I bought it passing cheap;
>   No doubt 'twas dearer to its first employer!
> I thought mortality did well to keep
>   Some mute memento of the Old Destroyer.
>
> Time was, some may have prized its blooming skin;
>   Here lips were woo'd, perhaps, in transport tender;
> Some may have chuck'd what was a dimpled chin,
>   And never had my doubt about its gender.
>
> .   .   .   .
>
> It may have held (to shoot some random shots)
>   Thy brains, Eliza Fry! or Baron Byron's;
> The wits of Nelly Gwynne or Doctor Watts—
>   Two quoted bards.   Two philanthropic sirens.
>
> But this, I trust, is clearly understood,
>   If man or woman, if adored or hated—
> Whoever own'd this Skull was not so good
>   Nor quite so bad as many may have stated.

Besides the playful humor of these poems, two
things especially are to be noted in them—individuality and directness of expression.   Whatever influence you may think you see here of some other poet,
Horace, or Béranger, or Gautier, or Thackeray,—
and the variety of these names shows the poet's
versatility,— you cannot doubt that these poems
are of a truth Mr. Locker's own, stamped with his

seal, marked with his image and superscription.
Here plainly is a man with a character of his own,
looking at life through his own eyes, now laughing
with hearty gayety, again smiling a sad smile :

> "*I still can laugh*" is still my boast,
>   But mirth has sounded gayer;
> And which provokes my laughter most,
>   The preacher or the player?
> Alack, I cannot laugh at what
>   Once made us laugh so freely;
> For Nestroy and Grassot are not,
>   And where is Mrs. Keeley?

Quite as noteworthy as the individuality of the
poet is his studied clearness.   There is never an
inversion or an involution ; the verse is as straightforward as prose, and as easy to be " understanded
of the people."   The rhythm flows freely ; the
rhymes are neat and novel, and never forced ; and
the manner never intrudes itself to the injury of
the matter.   But Mr. Locker is not like Théophile
Gautier, that Benvenuto Cellini of verse, nor like
the cunning artificers of Gautier's school—poets
who polish a poor little idea until they can see
themselves in it.   That he is ever going over his
work with the file any one can see who will compare the first stanzas of 'Geraldine and I,' and of
'A Garden Lyric'; but he never overweights his

verse with a gorgeous setting, from selfish delight
in the skill of his workmanship. Indeed, Mr. Locker
sometimes has carried his search for simplicity of
statement almost too far. But so many poets nowadays are as hard to understand as a Greek chorus,
that we ought to be thankful to one who takes
pains to be clear, and direct, and unaffected.

Affectation, indeed, is always a stumbling-block
in the path of the maker of *vers de société;* but in
'London Lyrics' there are no traces of any slip.
The poems are as simple and honest as the verse
is direct and clear. Nowhere is affectation more
easy than in addressing childhood; and, with the
exception of Victor Hugo and Longfellow, perhaps no poet of our day has written of children as
often as Mr. Locker. He has made a 'Rhyme of
One,' and 'Little Dinky,' a rhyme of less than one
(she is twelve weeks old). He has written 'To
Lina Oswald' (aged five years), and to 'Geraldine'
(who is fifteen); and 'Gertrude's Necklace' belonged to a maiden not much older. And all
these poems to the young reveal the subdued
humor and the worldly wit we have seen in the
others written for their elders and betters, their
pastors and masters, and they have even more of
delicate tenderness and of true sentiment tainted
by no trace of sentimentality.

5*

One of Mr. Locker's songs has a lyric grace and an evanescent´ sweetness, recalling Herrick or Suckling :

AT HER WINDOW.

Beating Heart! we come again
  Where my Love reposes;
This is Mabel's window-pane;
  These are Mabel's roses.

Is she nested ?   Does she kneel
  In the twilight stilly,
Lily-clad from throat to heel,
  She, my Virgin Lily ?

Soon the wan, the wistful stars,
  Fading, will forsake her;
Elves of light, on beamy bars,
  Whisper then, and wake her.

Let this friendly pebble plead
  At the flowery grating;
If she hear me, will she heed ?
  Mabel, I am waiting.

Mabel will be decked anon,
  Zoned in bride's apparel;
Happy zone ! oh, hark to yon
  Passion-shaken carol.

Sing thy song, thou tranced thrush,
  Pipe thy best, thy clearest;
Hush, her lattice moves, O, hush—
  Dearest Mabel !—dearest.

is not this a marvel of refinement and restraint?
It is as purely a lyric as the song of the thrush
itself. Especially in poems like this is it that Mr.
Locker is wholly other than Praed, with whom
people persist in linking him. He has at once a
finer vein of poetry and a broader vein of humor.
Perhaps, after all, humor is Mr. Locker's chief
characteristic,—a gentle humor, always under
control, and never boisterous or burly, yet frank
and free and full of mischief,—the humor of a
keen observer, who is at once a gentleman and a
poet. What, for example, can be more comic in
conception, or more clear-cut in execution, than
this?—

A TERRIBLE INFANT.

I recollect a nurse call'd Ann,
  Who carried me about the grass,
And one fine day a fine young man
  Came up and kissed the pretty lass.
She did not make the least objection!
    Thinks I—*"Aha!*
When I can talk I'll tell mamma!"
And that's my earliest recollection.

It is in this quality of humor mainly, and in the
fact that his verse is more individual than impersonal, that Mr. Locker's gifts differ from those of
Mr. Austin Dobson. There is no need to make

a comparison of Mr. Locker's work with Mr.
Dobson's ; and, at best, comparisons are futile.
Criticism is nowadays the tenth muse, and I am
sure that Mrs. Malaprop would say that comparisons do not become that young woman.   Suffice
it to state that Mr. Frederick Locker and Mr. Austin Dobson stand, each on his own ground, at the
head of the poets who sing of English society as it
is.   Mr. Locker is the elder, and it was to him
that Mr. Dobson dedicated his ' Proverbs in Porcelain,' in these lines :

> Is it to kindest friend I send
> 　This nosegay gathered new ?
> Or is it more to critic sure,
> 　To singer clear and true ?
> I know not which, indeed, nor need :
> 　All three I found — in you.

TWO LATTER-DAY LYRISTS.

II.

MR. AUSTIN DOBSON.

s Mr. Lang told us in his sympathetic paper on M. Théodore de Banville, some literary reputations are like the fairies in that they cannot cross running water.   Others again, it seems to me, are rather like the misty genii of the Arabian Nights, which loom highest when seen from afar.   Poe, for example, is more appreciated in England than at home; and Cooper is given a more lofty rank by French than by American critics.   In much the same manner, we note, Carlyle gained the ear of an American audience when he was not listened to with attention in Great Britain ; and the scattered verses of Praed were collected together for American admirers long before the appearance of an English edition. And so it is, I think, with Mr. Austin Dobson, whose position as a leader in one division of Eng-

lish poetry was recognized more immediately and
more unhesitatingly in these United States than
in his native Great Britain.   To Mr. Dobson the
young school of American writers of familiar
verse — to use Cowper's admirable phrase — look
up as to a master ; and his poems are read and
pondered and imitated by not a few of the more
promising of our younger poets.

Mr. Austin Dobson was born at Plymouth, Jan-
uary 18, 1840.   He comes of a family of civil
engineers, and it was as an engineer that his
grandfather, toward the end of the last century,
went to France, where he settled, and married a
French lady.   Among the earliest recollections of
Mr. Dobson's father was his arrival in Paris on
one side of the Seine as the Russians arrived on
the other.   This must have been in 1814.   But
the French boy had long become an English man
when the poet was born.   At the age of eight or
nine Austin Dobson was taken by his parents—
so a biographer tells us — " to Holyhead, in the
island of Anglesea; he was educated at Beaumaris,
at Coventry, and finally at Strasburg, whence he
returned, at the age of sixteen, with the inten-
tion of becoming a civil engineer."   But in December, 1856, he accepted an appointment in the
civil service, where he has remained ever since.

Thus he has been able to act on the advice of
Coleridge, often urged again by Dr. Holmes, to
the effect "that a literary man should have another calling." Dr. Holmes adds the sly suggestion that he should confine himself to it;
and this is what—for nearly ten years—Mr.
Dobson did. He dabbled a little in art, having,
like Théophile Gautier, the early ambition of becoming a painter. He learned to draw a little on
wood. He wrote a little, mostly in prose. In
fact, there are only four poems in the first edition
of ' Vignettes in Rhyme' which were written before 1868. It was in this year that *St. Paul's*
magazine was started by Anthony Trollope, an
editor at once sympathetic and severe; he appreciated good work, and was unsparing in the
kindly criticism which might make it better. In
St. Paul's, therefore, between March, 1868, and
March, 1874, appeared nearly twoscore of Mr.
Dobson's pieces, including some of his very best:
' Tu Quoque,' ' A Dialogue from Plato,' ' Une
Marquise,' ' An Autumn Idyll,' ' Dorothy,' ' A
Gentleman of the Old School,' ' Avice,'—with its
hazardous, bird-like effect, French in a way and in
exquisite taste,— and the subtle and pathetic
' Drama of the Doctor's Window.' In October,
1873, there was published the first edition of

'Vignettes in Rhyme,' and the poet received for the first time that general recognition which denies itself to the writer of verses scattered here and there, throughout magazines and newspapers. 'Vignettes in Rhyme' passed into its third edition ; and less than four years after its appearance Mr. Dobson made a second collection of his verses, published in May, 1877, as 'Proverbs in Porcelain.' From these two volumes the author made a selection, adding a few poems written since the appearance of the second book, and thus prepared the collective American volume, called 'Vignettes in Rhyme,' issued by Henry Holt & Co. in 1880, with a graceful and alluring introduction by Mr. Stedman. 'Old-World Idylls,' published in London in the fall of 1883, is based on this American selection of 1880. It has been followed by 'At the Sign of the Lyre,' which includes most of the poetry he wrote before 1885. Unfortunately we have not Mr. Dobson's complete poems even in these two collections, for his own fastidious taste has excluded poems which the less exacting reader had learned to like, and which the admirers of fine humorous verse will not willingly let die. Let us hope that there will be vouchsafed to us, in due time, a volume in which we may treasure Mr. Dobson's 'Complete Poetical Works.' Akin to the fastidiousness which rejects certain poems altogether—and quite as annoying to many—is the fastidiousness with which the poet is continually going over his verses with a file, polishing until they shine again, smoothing an asperity here, and there rubbing out a blot. This is always a dangerous pastime, and the poet is rarely well advised who attempts it, as all students of Lord Tennyson will bear witness. If the poet is athirst for perfection, he may lay his poems by for the Horatian space of nine years, but when they are once printed and published, he had best keep his hands off them. Of course the most of Mr. Dobson's alterations are unexceptionable improvements, yet there are a few that we reject with abhorrence.

Mr. Aldrich has said that Mr. Dobson "has the grace of Suckling and the finish of Herrick, and is easily master of both in metrical art." The beauty of his poetry is due in great measure to its lyric lightness. He has many lines and many whole poems which sing themselves into the memory, and cannot be thrust thence. Who that has made acquaintance with the 'Ladies of St. James's' can forget "Phillida, my Phillida"? And who cannot at will call up before him Autonoë and Rosina and Rose and all the other "damosels, blithe as the belted bees," whom the poet has set before us with so much breezy freshness? To know them is to love them, and to love the poet who has sung them into being. Next to the airy grace and the flowing and unfailing humor which inform all Mr. Dobson's poems, perhaps the quality which most deserves to be singled out is their frank and hearty wholesomeness. There is nothing sickly about them, or morbid, or perverse, as there is about so much contemporary British verse. Mr. Dobson is entirely free from the besetting sin of those minor poets who sing only in a minor key. He has no trace of affectation, and no taint of sentimentality. He is simple and sincere. His delicacy is manly, and not effeminate. There is a courtly dignity about all his work; and there is nowhere a hint of bad taste. Mr. Locker once spoke to me of the ' Unfinished Song,' and said that " the spirit is so beautiful"; and of a truth the spirit of all Mr. Dobson's work is beautiful. There is unfailing elevation. Mr. Dobson, in Joubert's phrase, never forgets that the lyre is a winged instrument. Here is a lyric, not one of his best known, and not in the style he most frequently attempts; but it is lifted out of commonplace, though the subject is hackneyed and worn; it soars, and sings as it soars, like the lark :

A SONG OF THE FOUR SEASONS.

When Spring comes laughing
    By vale and hill,
By wind-flower walking
    And daffodil,—
Sing stars of morning,
    Sing morning skies,
Sing blue of speedwell,
    And my Love's eyes.

When comes the Summer,
    Full-leaved and strong,
And gay birds gossip
    The orchard long,—
Sing hid, sweet honey
    That no bee sips;
Sing red, red roses,
    And my Love's lips.

When Autumn scatters
    The leaves again,
And piled sheaves bury
    The broad-wheeled wain,—
Sing flutes of harvest
    Where men rejoice;
Sing rounds of reapers,
    And my Love's voice.

> But when comes Winter
>   With hail and storm,
> And red fire roaring
>   And ingle warm,—
> Sing first sad going
>   Of friends that part;
> Then sing glad meeting,
>   And my Love's heart.

And with all this elevation and lyric lightness there is no lack of true pathos and genuine feeling for the lowly and the hopeless. More than once has Mr. Dobson expressed his sympathy for the striving, and especially for those strugglers who are handicapped in the race, and who eat their hearts in silent revolt against hard circumstances :

> Ah, Reader, ere you turn the page,
>   I leave you this for moral :—
> Remember those who tread life's stage
> With weary feet and scantest wage,
>   And ne'er a leaf for laurel.

The best of Mr. Dobson's poems result from a happy mingling of a broad and genial humanity with an extraordinarily fine artistic instinct. Just as Chopin declared that there were paintings at the sight of which he heard music, so it may be said that there are poems the hearing of which calls up a whole gallery of pictures. Side by side with

the purely lyric pieces are as many more as purely
pictorial.   The ' Curé's Progress,' for example, is
it not a like masterpiece of *genre?*   And the ballade ' On a Fan, that Belonged to the Marquise de
Pompadour,' with its wonderful movement and
spirit, and its apt suggestion of the courtiers and
courtesans "thronging the *Œil-de-Bœuf* through,"
is it not a perfect picture of

> The little great, the infinite small thing
> That ruled the hour when Louis Quinze was king?

This is a Fragonard, as the other is a Meissonnier.
It is not that the pathetic ' Story of Rosina ' has
for its hero François Boucher, or that other poems
abound in references to Watteau and Vanloo and
Hogarth ; it is not even that these references
are never at random, and always reveal an exact
knowledge and a nice appreciation ; it is rather
that Mr. Dobson is a painter at heart, in a degree
far from common even in these days of so-called
" word-painting."   He excels in the art of calling
up a scene before you by a few motions of his
magic pen ; and, once evoked, the scene abides
with you alway.   Mr. E. A. Abbey told me that
once in a nook of rural England he happened
suddenly on a sun-dial, and that lines from Mr.
Dobson's poem with that title rose to his lips at

once, and he felt as though nature had illustrated the poet.

This delightful effect is produced by no abuse of the customary devices of "word-painting," and by no squandering of "local color." On the contrary, Mr. Dobson is sober in his details, and rarely wastes time in description. He hits off a scene in a few happy strokes; there is no piling of a Pelion of adjectives on an Ossa of epithets. The picture is painted with the utmost economy of stroke. Mr. Dobson's method is like that of the etchers who work in the bath; his hand needs to be both swift and sure. Thus there is always a perfect unity of tone; there is always a shutting out of everything which is not essential to the picture. Consider the ballad of the Armada and the ' Ballad of Beau Brocade,'—a great favorite with Dr. Holmes, by the way,—and see if one is not as truly seventeenth century in thought and feeling as the other is eighteenth century, while both are thoroughly and robustly English. And how captivatingly Chinese are the verses about the "little blue mandarin" !

Of the French pictures I have already spoken, but inadequately, since I omitted to cite the ' Proverbs in Porcelain," which I should ascribe to a French poet, if I knew any Frenchman who could have accomplished so winning a commingling of banter and of grace, of high breeding and of playfulness.   How Roman are the various Horatian lyrics, and, above all, how Greek is 'Autonoë'! " 'Autonoë,'" as a friend writes me, "is the most purely beautiful of all Mr. Dobson's work.   It does not touch the heart, but it rests the spirit.   Most so-called 'classicism' shows us only the white temple, the clear high sky, the outward beauty of form and color.   This gives us the warm air of spring and the life that pulses in a girl's veins like the soft swelling of sap in a young tree.   This is the same feeling that raises 'As You Like It' above all pastoral poetry.   Our nineteenth century sensibilities are so played on by the troubles, the sorrows, the little vital needs and anxieties of the world around us, that sometimes it does us good to get out into the woods and fields of another world entirely, if only the atmosphere is not chilled and rarefied by the lack of the breath of humanity.   There are times when the 'Drama of the Doctor's Window' would excite us, but when 'Autonoë' would rest us—and not with a mere selfish intellectual rest."

About twelve years ago, early in 1876, Mr. Dobson began to turn his attention to what are generally known as the French forms of verse, although

they are not all of them French.   Oddly enough,
it happens that the introduction, at Mr. Dobson's
hands, of these French forms into English literature
is due—indirectly at least—to an American.   In
criticising Mr. Dobson's earlier verses in 'Victorian
Poets,' Mr. Stedman amiably admonished him that
"such a poet, to hold the hearts he has won, not
only must maintain his quality, but strive to vary
his style."   This warning from the American
critic, this particular Victorian poet, perhaps having some inner monitions of his own, took to
heart, and he began at once to cast about for some
new thing.   His first find was the 'Odes Funam-
bulesques' of M. Théodore de Banville, the reviver
of the triolet, the rondeau, and the ballade.   Here
was a new thing—a truly new thing, since it was
avowedly an old thing.   Mr. Dobson had written
a set of triolets already, in 1874; it was in May,
1876, that he published the first original ballade
ever written in English, the firm and vigorous
'Prodigals,' slightly irregular in its repetition of
rhymes, but none the less a most honorable beginning.   Almost at the same time he attempted also
the rondeau and the rondel.   A year later, in May,
1877, he published his second volume of verse,
'Proverbs in Porcelain,' and this, followed almost
immediately by Mr. Gosse's easy and learned 'Plea

for Certain Exotic Forms of Verse,' in the *Cornhill Magazine* of July, 1877, drew general attention to the new weapons with which the poet's armory had been enriched.

It would be idle to maintain that they have met with universal acceptance. Mr. Stedman, when introducing the author to the American public, confesses that he is not certain whether to thank Mr. Dobson or to condole with him on bringing into fashion the ballade and the rondeau and its fellows. Perhaps this was partly due to the sudden rush of versifiers who wreaked themselves on these forms, and did their little best to bring them into disrepute. Perhaps it was due to a wider dislike of metrical limitations and of all that tempts the poet to expend any of his strength otherwise than on the straightforward delivery of his message.

Yet rhyme itself, as M. Edmond Schérer tells us, "is a very curious thing, and it is a very complex pleasure which it gives. We do not like to confess how great in every art is the share of difficulty vanquished, and yet it is difficulty vanquished which gives the impression of surprise, and it is surprise which gives interest; it is the unexpected which gives us the sense of the writer's power." The testimony of Sidney Lanier—an untiring student of his art and its science—is to

6

the same effect: "It is only cleverness and small talent which is afraid of its spontaneity; the genius, the great artist, is forever ravenous after new forms, after technic; he will follow you to the ends of the earth, if you will enlarge his artistic science, if you will give him a fresh form." Finally, the fact remains that great poets—Dante, Milton, Wordsworth—have not scorned the sonnet's scanty plot of ground; and the sonnet is as rigid and quite as difficult, if you play the game fairly, as either the ballade or the rondeau. The rondeau and rondel, have they not a charm of their own when handled by a genuine poet? And the ballade,—that little three-act comedy in rhyme with its epigram-epilogue of an envoy,—has it not both variety and dignity?

For the Malayan pantoum, as for the Franco-Italian sestina, with their enervating and exasperating monotony, there is really nothing to be said. And perhaps there is no need to say much for the tiny triolet, effective as it may be for occasional epigram, or for the elaborate and stately chant-royal, which is a feat of skill, no more and no less; that Mr. Dobson has done it as well as he has suggests, perhaps, only the pertinent query as to whether it was well worth doing. Perhaps no more must be said in favor of the dainty little villanelle—a form which exists under the greatest disadvantage, since the first and typical specimen, the ever fresh and graceful 'J'ai perdu ma tourterelle' of Passerat, remains to this day unsurpassable and unapproached. But the rondeau and rondel carry no such weight, and in the hands of a master of metres they are capable of being filled with a simple beauty most enjoyable. What could be more delicate, more pensive, more charming than this rondel of Mr. Dobson's?—

THE WANDERER.

Love comes back to his vacant dwelling,—
   The old, old Love that we knew of yore!
   We see him stand by the open door,
With his great eyes sad, and his bosom swelling.

He makes as though in our arms repelling,
   He fain would lie as he lay before;—
   Love comes back to his vacant dwelling,—
The old, old Love that we knew of yore!

Ah, who shall help us from over-telling
   That sweet forgotten, forbidden lore!
   E'en as we doubt in our heart once more,
With a rush of tears to our eyelids welling,
Love comes back to his vacant dwelling.

The ballade, however, is by far the best of all these forms. I hold it second to the sonnet alone,

and for some purposes superior even to the sonnet.
It is fair to say that it is the only one of the French
poems which in France itself has held its own
against the Italian sonnet. The instrument used
by Clément Marot, by Villon,—that "voice out
of the slums of Paris," as Mr. Matthew Arnold
called him,—by La Fontaine, and in later times by
Albert Glatigny and Théodore de Banville, is surely
worthy of honor. In Villon's hands it has dignity
and depth, in Glatigny's it has pathos, and in Marot's,
in Mr. Dobson's, and in Mr. Lang's it has playfulness
and gayety. I believe Mr. Dobson himself likes the
'Ballade of Imitation' better than any of his other
ballades, while I confess my own preference for the
'Ballade of Prose and Rhyme,' the only *ballade à
double refrain* worthy to be set alongside Clément
Marot's 'Frère Lubin.' It is almost too familiar to
quote here at length, and yet it must be quoted perforce, for nohow else can I get the testimony of my
best witness fully before the jury:

THE BALLADE OF PROSE AND RHYME.

(Ballade à Double Refrain.)

When the ways are heavy with mire and rut,
  In November fogs, in December snows,
When the North Wind howls, and the doors are shut,—
  There is place and enough for the pains of prose;

But whenever a scent from the whitethorn blows,
And the jasmine-stars at the casement climb,
  And a Rosalind-face at the lattice shows,
Then hey!—for the ripple of laughing rhyme!

When the brain gets dry as an empty nut,
  When the reason stands on its squarest toes,
When the mind (like a beard) has a "formal cut,"—
  There is place and enough for the pains of prose;
  But whenever the May-blood stirs and glows,
And the young year draws to the "golden prime"
  And Sir Romeo sticks in his ear a rose,—
Then hey!—for the ripple of laughing rhyme!

In a theme where the thoughts have a pedant-strut,
  In a changing quarrel of "Ayes" and "Noes,"
In a starched procession of "If" and "But,"—
  There is place and enough for the pains of prose;
  But whenever a soft glance softer grows
And the light hours dance to the trysting-time,
  And the secret is told "that no one knows,"—
Then hey!—for the ripple of laughing rhyme!

ENVOY.

In the work-a-day world,—for its needs and woes,
There is place and enough for the pains of prose;
But whenever the May-bells clash and chime,
Then hey!—for the ripple of laughing rhyme!

It seems to me that in these poems Mr. Dobson
proves that the rondel at its best and the ballade
at its finest, belong to the poetry of feeling and

not to the poetry of ingenuity. It seems to me, also, that the poet has been helped by his restrictions. Here are cases where a faith in these forms is justified by works. We may ask, fairly enough, whether either of these poems would be as good in any other shape. From the compression enforced by the rules, they have gained in compactness, and therefore in swiftness. They are, in Miltonic phrase, '' woven close, both matter, form, and style.''

It is to Mr. Dobson primarily and to his fellow-workers that the credit is due of acclimatizing these exotic metres in English literature. It is not that he was absolutely the earliest to write them in English — excepting only the ballade, of which the 'Prodigals' was the first. Chaucer wrote rondels, the elder Wyatt rondeaus, and Patrick Carey, about 1651, was guilty of devotional triolets! But England was not then ready for the conquest, and the forms crossed the Channel, like the Norseman, just to set foot on land and then away again. Even in France they had faded out of sight. Molière speaks slightingly of ballades as old-fashioned. Only in our own times, since M. de Banville set the example, has the true form been understood. Wyatt's rondeaus were printed as though they were defective sonnets. Both

Longfellow and Bryant translated Clément Marot's
'Frère Lubin,' and neither of them knew it was a
ballade à double refrain.   Nor is Rossetti's noble
rendering of Villon's famous 'Ballade of Dead
Ladies' accurately formal.   Mr. Lang, in his 'Bal-
lads and Lyrics of Old France' (1872), was plainly
on the right track, but he failed then to reach the
goal.   At last the time was ripe.

It was doubtless again due to Mr. Stedman's
warning that, although there is no work which
when well done secures a welcome as instant as
vers de société, there is also "none from which the
world so lightly turns upon the arrival of a new
favorite with a different note,"—it was this wise
warning which led Mr. Dobson to vary his style,
not only with the revival of the French forms, but
also with fables and with a slight attempt at the
drama — in so far as the dainty and delicate
'Proverbs in Porcelain' are substantial enough to
be called dramatic.   Like John Gay and like the
late John G. Saxe, Mr. Dobson took to rhyming
fables after making a mark by more characteristic
verse.   And Mr. Dobson's fables, good as they
are, and pertinent and brightsome as they needs
must be, since he wrote them, are like Gay's and
Saxe's in that they are not their author's best
work.   The fault plainly is in the fable form,

if Mr. Dobson's fables are not as entertaining as his other poems; at any rate, I am free to confess that I like his other work better.

I have to confess, also, with great doubt and diffidence, that the half-dozen little dialogues called 'Proverbs in Porcelain,' airy as they are and exquisite, are less favorites with me than they are with critics whose taste I cannot but think finer than mine — Mr. Aldrich, for instance, and Mr. Stedman. I am inclined to believe I like them less because they assume a dramatic form without warrant. The essence of the drama is action, and in these beautiful and witty playlets there is but the ghost of an action. I doubt not that I am unfair to these dialogues, and that my attitude toward them is that of the dramatic critic rather than that of the critic of poetry pure and simple. But that is their own fault for assuming a virtue they have not. To counterbalance this harsh treatment of the 'Proverbs in Porcelain,' I must declare that I take more pleasure in 'A Virtuoso' than do most of Mr. Dobson's admirers, and for the same reason. I find in 'A Virtuoso' all the condensed compactness of the best stage dialogue, where a phrase has to be stripped to run for its life. To be read quickly by the fireside, 'A Virtuoso' may seem forced; but to be acted or

recited, it is just right.   I see in this cold and cutting poem, masterly in its synthesis of selfish
symptoms, a regard for theatrical perspective, and
a selection and a heightening of effect in accordance with the needs of the stage, which I confess
I fail to find in the seemingly more dramatic
'Proverbs in Porcelain.'   Most people, however,
liking Mr. Dobson mainly for playful tenderness
and tender playfulness, dislike the marble hard-
ness of 'A Virtuoso,' just as they are annoyed by
the tone of 'A Love-letter,' one of the poet's
cleverest pieces.   If Mr. Dobson yielded to the
likes and dislikes of his admirers he would soon
sink into sentimentality, and he would never dare
to write as funny as he can.   There are readers
who are shocked and pained when they discover
the non-existence of 'Dorothy.'

After all, this is perhaps the highest compliment that readers can pay the writer, when they
enter so heartily into his creations that they revolt
against any trick he may play upon them.   And
in these days of haste without rest, it ill becomes
us to fling the first stone at an author who is
enamored of elusive perfection and who is willing
to spare no pains to give us his best and only his
best.   He may be thankful that he is not as infer-
tile on the one hand as Waller, who was "the

6*

greater part of a summer correcting *ten* lines for Her Grace of York's copy of Tasso," or as reckless on the other hand as Martial, who disdained to elaborate :

> Turpe est difficile habere nugas
> Et stultus labor est ineptiarum.

Not infrequently do we find Mr. Frederick Locker and Mr. Dobson classed together as though their work was fundamentally of the same kind. The present writer has to plead guilty to the charge of inadvertently and inaccurately linking the two names in critical discussion. The likeness is accidental rather than essential, and the hasty conjunction is due, perhaps, more to the fact that they are friends, and that they both write what has to be called *vers de société*, than to any real likeness between their works. The fact is, the more clearly we define, and the more precisely we limit the phrase *vers de société*, the more exactly do we find the best and most characteristic of Mr. Locker's poems agreeing with the definition and lying at ease within the limitation ; while the best and most characteristic of Mr. Dobson's poems would be left outside. In his criticism of Praed's work prefixed to the selection from his poems in the fourth volume of Mr. Ward's 'English Poets' Mr.

Dobson declares that " as a writer of ' society verse '
in its exacter sense, Praed was justly acknowledged to be supreme," and then he adds, "We
say 'exacter sense' because it has of late become
the fashion to apply this vague term in the vaguest
way possible so as to include almost all verse but
the highest and the lowest. This is manifestly a
mistake. Society verse as Praed understood it,
and as we understand it in Praed, treats almost ex-
clusively of the *votum, timor, ira, voluptas* (and
especially the *voluptas)* of that charmed circle of
uncertain limits known conventionally as 'good society'—those latter-day Athenians who, in town
and country, spend their time in telling or hearing
some new thing, and whose graver and deeper
impulses are subordinated to a code of artificial
manners." Of these it is indisputable that Mr.
Locker is, as Praed was, the laureate-elect, and
that " the narrow world in which they move is the
main haunt and region of his song." Mr. Locker
writes as one to the manner born, and nowhere
reveals the touch of the parvenu which betrayed
Praed now and again. In the exact sense of the
phrase, Mr. Locker, like Praed, is the poet of society, which Mr. Dobson is not—because, for one
thing, we may doubt whether society is of quite so
much interest or importance or significance to him

as to the author of 'London Lyrics.' The distinction is evasive, and has to be suggested rather than said ; but it is none the less real and vital. It is, perhaps, rather that Mr. Dobson is more a man of letters, while Mr. Locker is more a man of the world. Certainly Mr. Dobson has a more consciously literary style than Mr. Locker, a style less simple and less direct. Henri Monnier would say that Mr. Dobson had more *mots d'auteur*. Admirable as is Mr. Dobson's verse, it has not the condensed clearness nor the incisive vigor of Mr. Locker's. One inclines to the opinion that the author of 'London Lyrics' is willing to make more sacrifices for vernacular terseness than the author of 'Vignettes in Rhyme.' It is not that Mr. Dobson is one of the poets who keep their choicest wares locked in an inner safe guarded by heavy bolts, and to whose wisdom no man may help himself unless he has the mystic letters which unlock the massive doors, but he is not quite willing to be simple to the point of bareness as is Mr. Locker, who wears his heart upon his sleeve. In some things Mr. Locker is like Mr. du Maurier, even in the little Gallic twist, while Mr. Dobson is rather like Randolph Caldecott or our own Abbey, with the quaint Englishry of whose style Mr. Dobson's has much in common. Yet after say-

ing this I feel inclined to take it all back, for I recall
together 'This was the Pompadour's fan' and
'This is Gerty's glove'—and here it is Mr. Dobson who is brilliant and French and Mr. Locker
who is more simple in sentiment and more English. Yet again it is the worldly-minded Mr.
Locker who declares that

> The world's as ugly, aye, as sin —
> And nearly as delightful,—

a sentiment wholly foreign to Mr. Dobson's feelings. This suggests that there is a certain town
stamp in the appropriately named 'London Lyrics'
not to be seen in ' Vignettes in Rhyme,' some of
which are vignettes from rural nature. But both
books are boons to be thankful for. Both are
havens of rest in days of depression ; both have a
joyousness most tonic and wholesome in these
days when the general tone of literature is gray ;
both preach the gospel of sanity, and both may
serve as antiseptics against sentimental decay.

Here occasion serves to say that each of these
masters of what Dr. Johnson, while declaring its
difficulty, called "easy verse," has set forth his
views of the art of writing *vers de société*. Mr.
Locker made his declaration of faith in the admirable preface, all too brief, to the selection of *vers*

de société and *vers d'occasion*, which he published
in 1867 as 'Lyra Elegantiarum.' Mr. Dobson, at
the request of the present writer, drew up a code
for the composition of familiar verse. Here are
Mr. Dobson's 'Twelve Good Rules':

    I. Never be vulgar.
   II. Avoid slang and puns.
  III. Avoid inversions.
  IV. Be sparing of long words.
   V. Be colloquial, but not commonplace.
  VI. Choose the lightest and brightest of measures.
 VII. Let the rhymes be frequent, but not forced.
VIII. Let them be rigorously exact to the ear.
  IX. Be as witty as you like.
   X. Be serious by accident.
  XI. Be pathetic with the greatest discretion.
 XII. Never ask if the writer of these rules has observed them
     himself.

Mr. Dobson has not confined his labors in prose
to the canons of familiar verse. Although it is
as a poet that he is most widely known, his prose
has qualities of its own. Besides scattering magazine articles, it includes half a dozen apt and alert
criticisms in Mr. Ward's 'English Poets,' the final
chapter in Mr. Lang's little book on the 'Library,'
and prefaces to a fac-simile reprint of 'Robin-
son Crusoe,' and to the selection from Herrick's

poems, illustrated by Mr. Abbey with such abundant sympathy and such delightful grace and fancy. More important than these are the volumes in which Mr. Dobson has given us selections from the best of the ' Eighteenth Century Essays,' and in which he has introduced and annotated the ' Fables ' of John Gay, the ' Poems ' and 'Vicar of Wakefield ' of Oliver Goldsmith, the ' Essays ' of Richard Steele, and the ' Barbier de Séville ' of Beaumarchais.

Still more important are the biographical sketches of his favorite Hogarth, and of Bewick and his pupils ; and the lives of Fielding, Steele, and Goldsmith. It was to Mr. Dobson's biography that Mr. Lowell referred when he unveiled Miss Margaret Thomas's bust of Fielding in the Somersetshire hall. In the course of his speech, as rich and eloquent as only his speeches are, Mr. Lowell said that " Mr. Austin Dobson has done, perhaps, as true a service as one man of letters ever did to another, by reducing what little is known of the life of Fielding from chaos to coherence, by ridding it of fable, by correcting and coördinating dates, by cross-examining tradition till it stammeringly confessed that it had no visible means of subsistence, and has thus enabled us to get some authentic glimpse of the man as he really was. Lessing

gives the title of 'Rescues' to the essays in which
he strove to rehabilitate such authors as had been,
in his judgment, unjustly treated by their contemporaries, and Mr. Dobson's essay deserves to be
reckoned in the same category. , He has rescued
the body of Fielding from beneath the swinish
hoofs which were trampling it as once they tram-
pled the Knight of La Mancha, whom Fielding so
heartily admired."

It has been well said that the study of practice
of verse is the best of trainings for the writing of
prose.   Mr. Dobson's prose style is firm and precise; it has no taint of the Corinthian luxuriance
which Mr. Matthew Arnold has castigated, or of
the passionate emphasis which passes for criticism in some quarters.   His ideal in prose writing is a style exact and cool and straightforward.
Sometimes the reader might like a little more
glow.   It is not that his prose style is sapless,
for it has life; it is rather that it is generally cut-
and-dried of malice prepense.   He can write
prose with more color and more heat when he
chooses, as he who will may see in the par-
agraphs of the preface to Mr. Abbey's 'Herrick.'
In general, however, Mr. Dobson forgets that he
is a poet when he takes up his pen to write prose,
and he remembers only that he is an antiquary

and an investigator. In fact, his prose is the prose
of a scientific historian; and Mr. Dobson has the
scientific virtues,—the passion for exactness, the
untiring patience in research, and the unwilling-
ness to set down anything which has not been
proved. If we apply De Quincey's classification,
we should declare that Mr. Dobson's poetry—like
all true poetry—belongs to the literature of
power, while his prose belongs to the literature
of knowledge.

It is to be remarked, also, that the poet sometimes remembers that he is an antiquary, also.
Here Mr. Dobson is not unlike Walter Scott, who
was also an antiquary-poet, with a strong love for
the past, and a gift for making dead figures start
to life at his bidding. Much of Mr. Dobson's
poetry is like his prose in that it is based on research. His learning in the manners and customs
of past times is most minute. Especially rich is
his knowledge of the people and of the vocabulary
of the eighteenth century. This is the result of
indefatigable delving in the records of the past.
His acquaintance with the ways and words of the
contemporaries of Steele and of Fielding and of
Hogarth is as thorough as Lord Tennyson's knowledge of botany, for instance; and it is the proof
of as much minute observation. Although Mr.

Dobson disdains all second-hand information, and likes to verify facts for himself, he never lets his learning burden his verse. That runs as freely and as trippingly as though the seeking of the facts on which it might be founded had not been a labor of love, for which no toil was too great. The 'Ballad of Beau Brocade' is a strong and simple tale, seemingly calling for no special study; but it does not contain a single word not in actual use at the time of the guide-book where it germinated, and in print in the pages of the *Gentleman's Magazine* of that reign. In like manner, in the noble and virile ballade of the Armada, which the Virgin Queen might have joyed to accept, there is no single word not in Gervase Markham.

Writing always out of the fulness of knowledge, there is nowhere anything amateurish, and there is always a perfect certainty of touch. His work—as Mr. W. C. Brownell has told us—is "as natural an outgrowth as Lamb's." And he is like Lamb in that capacity for taking infinite pains which has been held the true trade-mark of genius. He is like Lamb, again, in that he has resolutely recognized his limitations. Ruler of his own territory, he has carefully refrained from crossing his neighbor's boundaries. Indeed, he is as admirable an instance as one could wish of the exactness of Swift's dictum, "It is an uncontrolled truth that no man ever made an ill figure who understood his own talents, nor a good one who mistook them."

THE SONGS OF THE CIVIL WAR.

NATIONAL hymn is one of the things which cannot be made to order. No man has ever yet sat him down and taken up his pen and said, "I will write a national hymn," and composed either words or music which a nation was willing to take for its own. The making of the song of the people is a happy accident, not to be accomplished by taking thought. It must be the result of fiery feeling long confined, and suddenly finding vent in burning words or moving strains. Sometimes the heat and the pressure of emotion have been fierce enough and intense enough to call forth at once both words and music, and to weld them together indissolubly once and for all. Almost always the maker of the song does not suspect the abiding value of his work; he has wrought unconsciously, moved by a power within; he has written for immediate

relief to himself, and with no thought of fame or
the future ; he has builded better than he knew.
The great national lyric is the result of the conjunction of the hour and the man. Monarchs cannot command it, and even poets are often powerless
to achieve it. No one of the great national hymns
has been written by a great poet. But for his
single immortal lyric, neither the author of the
'Marseillaise' nor the author of the 'Wacht am
Rhein' would have his line in the biographical dic-
tionaries. But when a song has once taken root
in the hearts of a people, time itself is powerless
against it. The flat and feeble 'Partant pour la
Syrie,' which a filial fiat made the hymn of imperial France, had to give way to the strong and
virile notes of the 'Marseillaise,' when need was
to arouse the martial spirit of the French in 1870.
The noble measures of ' God Save the King,' as
simple and dignified a national hymn as any country can boast, lift up the hearts of the English
people ; and the brisk tune of the ' British Grena-
diers' has swept away many a man into the ranks
of the recruiting regiment. The English are rich
in war tunes ; and the pathetic 'Girl I left behind
me' encourages and sustains both those who go to
the front and those who remain at home. Here
in the United States we have no 'Marseillaise,' no

'God Save the King,' no 'Wacht am Rhein'; we have but 'Yankee Doodle' and the 'Star-spangled Banner.' More than one enterprising poet, and more than one aspiring musician, has volunteered to take the contract to supply the deficiency; as yet no one has succeeded. 'Yankee Doodle' we got during the Revolution, and the 'Star-spangled Banner' was the gift of the War of 1812; from the Civil War we have received at least two war songs which, as war songs simply, are stronger and finer than either of these—'John Brown's Body' and 'Marching Through Georgia.'

Of the lyrical outburst which the war called forth but little trace is now to be detected in literature except by special students. In most cases neither words nor music have had vitality enough to survive a quarter of a century. Chiefly, indeed, two things only survive, one Southern and the other Northern; one a war-cry in verse, the other a martial tune : one is the lyric 'My Maryland,' and the other is the marching song 'John Brown's Body.' The origin and development of the latter, the rude chant to which a million of the soldiers of the Union kept time, is uncertain and involved in dispute. The history of the former may be declared exactly, and by the courtesy of those who did the deed—for the making of a war song is of a

truth a deed at arms—I am enabled to state fully
the circumstances under which it was written, set
to music, and first sung before the soldiers of the
South.

'My Maryland' was written by Mr. James R.
Randall, a native of Baltimore, and now residing
in Augusta, Georgia.   The poet was a professor
of English literature and the classics in Poydras
College at Pointe Coupée, on the Fausse Rivière,
in Louisiana, about seven miles from the Mississippi; and there in April, 1861, he read in the
New Orleans *Delta* the news of the attack on the
Massachusetts troops as they passed through Baltimore.   "This account excited me greatly," Mr.
Randall wrote in answer to my request for information; "I had long been absent from my native
city, and the startling event there inflamed my
mind.   That night I could not sleep, for my
nerves were all unstrung, and I could not dismiss
what I had read in the paper from my mind.
About midnight I rose, lit a candle, and went to
my desk.   Some powerful spirit appeared to pos-
sess me, and almost involuntarily I proceeded to
write the song of 'My Maryland.'   I remember
that the idea appeared to first take shape as music
in the brain—some wild air that I cannot now recall.   The whole poem was dashed off rapidly

when once begun.   It was not composed in cold
blood, but under what may be called a conflagration
of the senses, if not an inspiration of the intellect.
I was stirred to a desire for some way linking my
name with that of my native State, if not ' with
my land's language.'   But I never expected to do
this with one single, supreme effort, and no one
was more surprised than I was at the widespread
and instantaneous popularity of the lyric I had been
so strangely stimulated to write."   Mr. Randall
read the poem the next morning to the college boys,
and at their suggestion sent it to the *Delta*, in which
it was first printed, and from which it was copied
into nearly every Southern journal.   "I did not
concern myself much about it, but very soon,
from all parts of the country, there was borne to
me, in my remote place of residence, evidence
that I had made a great hit, and that, whatever
might be the fate of the Confederacy, the song
would survive it."

Published in the last days of April, 1861, when
every eye was fixed on the border States, the stirring stanzas of the Tyrtæan bard appeared in the
very nick of time.   There is often a feeling afloat
in the minds of men, undefined and vague for
want of one to give it form, and held in solution,
as it were, until a chance word dropped in the ear

of a poet suddenly crystallizes this feeling into
song, in which all may see clearly and sharply reflected what in their own thought was shapeless
and hazy.   It was Mr. Randall's good fortune to
be the instrument through which the South spoke.
By a natural reaction his burning lines helped to
fire the Southern heart.   To do their work well,
his words needed to be wedded to music.   Unlike
the authors of the ' Star-spangled Banner ' and the
' Marseillaise,' the author of ' My Maryland ' had
not written it to fit a tune already familiar.   It
was left for a lady of Baltimore to lend the lyric
the musical wings it needed to enable it to reach
every camp-fire of the Southern armies.   To the
courtesy of this lady, then Miss Hetty Cary, and
now the wife of Professor H. Newell Martin, of
Johns Hopkins University, I am indebted for a pict-
uresque description of the marriage of the words
to the music, and of the first singing of the song
before the Southern troops.

The house of Mrs. Martin's father was the
headquarters for the Southern sympathizers of Baltimore.   Correspondence, money, clothing, sup-
plies of all kinds went thence through the lines to
the young men of the city who had joined the
Confederate army.   '' The enthusiasm of the girls
who worked and of the ' boys ' who watched for

7

their chance to slip through the lines to Dixie's land found vent and inspiration in such patriotic songs as could be made or adapted to suit our needs. The glee club was to hold its meeting in our parlors one evening early in June, and my sister, Miss Jenny Cary, being the only musical member of the family, had charge of the programme on the occasion. With a school-girl's eagerness to score a success, she resolved to secure some new and ardent expression of feelings that by this time were wrought up to the point of explosion. In vain she searched through her stock of songs and airs—nothing seemed intense enough to suit her. Aroused by her tone of despair, I came to the rescue with the suggestion that she should adapt the words of 'Maryland, my Maryland,' which had been constantly on my lips since the appearance of the lyric a few days before in the South. I produced the paper and began declaiming the verses. 'Lauriger Horatius,' she exclaimed, and in a flash the immortal song found voice in the stirring air so perfectly adapted to it. That night, when her contralto voice rang out the stanzas, the refrain rolled forth from every throat present without pause or preparation ; and the enthusiasm communicated itself with such effect to a crowd assembled beneath our open windows as to endanger seriously the liberties of the party."

'Lauriger Horatius' has long been a favorite
college song, and it had been introduced into the
Cary household by Mr. Burton N. Harrison, then a
Yale student.   The air to which it is sung is used
also for a lovely German lyric, 'Tannenbaum, O
Tannenbaum,' which Longfellow has translated ' O
Hemlock Tree.'   The transmigration of tunes is too
large and fertile a subject for me to do more here
than refer to it.   The taking of the air of a jovial
college song to use as the setting of a fiery war-
lyric may seem strange and curious, but only to
those who are not familiar with the adventures
and transformations a tune is often made to undergo.   Hopkinson's 'Hail Columbia!' for example,
was written to the tune of the 'President's March,'
just as Mrs. Howe's 'Battle Hymn of the Republic'
was written to 'John Brown's Body.'   The 'Wearing of the Green,' of the Irishman, is sung to the
same air as the 'Benny Havens, O !' of the West-
Pointer.   The 'Star-spangled Banner' has to make
shift with the second-hand music of 'Anacreon in
Heaven,' while our other national air, 'Yankee
Doodle,' uses over the notes of an old English
nursery rhyme, 'Lucy Locket,' once a personal
lampoon in the days of the 'Beggars' Opera,' and
now surviving in the 'Baby's Opera' of Mr. Walter
Crane.   'My Country, 'tis of Thee,' is set to the

truly British tune of 'God Save the King,' the origin of which is doubtful, as it is claimed by the French and the Germans as well as the English. In the hour of battle a war-tune is subject to the right of capture, and, like the cannon taken from the enemy, it is turned against its maker.

To return to 'My Maryland':—a few weeks after the welding of the words and the music, Mrs. Martin, with her husband and sister, went through the lines, convoying several trunks full of military clothing, and wearing concealed about her person a flag bearing the arms of Maryland, a gift from the ladies of Baltimore to the Maryland troops in the Confederate army. In consequence of reports which were borne back to the Union authorities the ladies were forbidden to return. "We were living," so Mrs. Martin writes me, "in Virginia in exile, when, shortly after the battle of Manassas, General Beauregard, hearing of our labors and sufferings in behalf of the Marylanders who had already done such gallant service in his command, invited us to visit them at his headquarters near Fairfax Court House, sending a pass and an escort for us, and the friends by whom we should be accompanied. Our party encamped the first night in tents prepared for us at Manassas, with my kinsman, Captain Sterrell, who was in charge of the fortifications there.   We were serenaded by the famous Washington Artillery of New Orleans, aided by all the fine voices within reach.   Captain Sterrell expressed our thanks, and asked if there were any service we might render in return. 'Let us hear a woman's voice,' was the cry which arose in response.   And, standing in the tent-door, under cover of the darkness, my sister sang 'My Maryland!'   This, I believe, was the birth of the song in the army.   The refrain was speedily caught up and tossed back to us from hundreds of rebel throats.   As the last notes died away there surged forth from the gathering throng a wild shout— '*We* will break her chains !   She *shall* be be free !   She *shall* be free !   Three cheers and a tiger for Maryland ! '   And they were given with a will.   There was not a dry eye in the tent, and, we were told the next day, not a cap with a rim on it in camp.   Nothing could have kept Mr. Randall's verses from living and growing into a power.   To us fell the happy chance of first giving them voice. In a few weeks 'My Maryland !' had found its way to the hearts of our whole people, and become a great national song."

I wish I could call as charming and as striking a witness to set forth the origin of 'John Brown's Body.'   The genesis of both words and music is

obscure and involved.   The raw facts of historical
criticism—names, places, dates—are deficient.
The martial hymn has been called a spontaneous
generation of the uprising of the North—a self-
made song, which sang itself into being of its own
accord.   Some have treated it as a sudden evolution from the inner consciousness of the early
soldiers all aglow with free-soil enthusiasm; and
these speak of it as springing, like Minerva from
the head of Jove, full armed and mature.   Others
have more happily likened it to Topsy, in that it
never was born, it growed; and this latter theory
has the support of the facts as far as they can be
disentangled from a maze of fiction and legend.
A tentative and conjectural reconstruction of the
story of the song is all I dare venture upon; and I
stand corrected in anticipation.

The Latter-day Saints of 1843 had a camp-
meeting song referring to the Second Advent,
'Say, brothers, will you meet us?'   Whence this
tune came, and whether or not it is a native negro
air, I have been wholly unable to discover.   I can
be certain only of its later popularity.   Within
fifteen years it spread over the country.   Mr. C.
G. Leland says that the song "was a great favorite
with John Brown" and that "it was sung with an
improvised variation adapted to John Brown him-

self by those who were in his funeral as it passed through the streets of New-York."

John Brown was hanged in December, 1859. A little more than a year later the report of the shot against the flag at Sumter rang through all the States and startled the blood of every man in the nation. Then suddenly the new song of ' John Brown's Body ' sprang into being. It was the song of the hour. There was a special taunt to the South in the use of the name of the martyr of abolition, while to the North that name was as a slogan. As the poet — a prophet again, for once — had written when John Brown was yet alive, though condemned to death:

But, Virginians, don't do it ! for I tell you that the flagon,
    Filled with blood of old Brown's offspring, was first poured
        by Southern hands ;
And each drop from old Brown's life-veins, like the red gore
        of the dragon,
    May spring up a vengeful fury, hissing through your slave-
        worn lands!
             And old Brown,
           Osawatomie Brown,
May trouble you more than ever, when you've nailed his
    coffin down !

The putting together of the rude version first sung in the rising heat of the war fever, the fitting

of plain rough words to the tune of 'Say, brothers,
will you meet us?'—the tune of which was
made more marked, and modified to a march—
seems to have been done by a little knot of men
in the second battalion, the Tigers, a Massachusetts command quartered at Fort Warren, in Boston Harbor, in April, 1861, just at the time when
'My Maryland' was getting itself sung at the
South.   A writer in the Boston *Herald* says that
"the manner in which 'the old tune' was taken
to Fort Warren was simple.   Two members of
the Tigers were present at a camp-meeting service
in a small town in New Hampshire during the fall
preceding the occupancy of the fort," and they
learned the air there.   Their names were Purring-
ton and Brown ; and when the Tigers went to
the fort and joined the 12th regiment, these two
vocalists took unto themselves two more, Edgerly
and Greenleaf—the latter a professional musician.
By this quartet the rudimentary John Brown song
seems to have been evolved out of the old camp-
meeting lyric.   Beyond all question it was the
Webster regiment which first adopted 'John
Brown's Body' as a marching song.   The soldiers
of this regiment sang it as they marched down
Broadway, in New-York, July 24, 1861, on their
way from Boston to the front.   They sang it

incessantly until August, 1862, when Colonel
Webster died, and when the tune had been taken
up by the nation at large and hundreds of thousands of soldiers were marching forward to the
fight with the name of John Brown on their lips.

There was a majestic simplicity in the rhythm
like the beating of mighty hammers. In the beginning the words were bare to the verge of barren-
ness. There was no lack of poets to fill them out.
Henry Howard Brownell, the singer of the 'Bay
Fight' and the 'River Fight,' skilfully utilized the accepted lines, which he enriched with a deeper meaning. Then Mrs. Howe wrote her 'Battle Hymn of
the Republic,' perhaps the most resonant and ele-
vated of the poems of American patriotism. Its
religious fervor was in consonance with the camp-
meeting origin of the song, and even more fully
with the intense feeling of the time. Of late the
air has been taken again by Mr. William Morris,
poet and socialist, decorator and reformer, as the
one to which shall be sung his eloquent and stirring 'March of the Workers.'

Curiously enough, the history of 'Dixie' is not
at all unlike the history of 'John Brown's Body.'
'Dixie' was composed in 1859, by Mr. Dan D.
Emmett, as a "walk-around" for Bryant's minstrels, then performing at Mechanics' Hall in New-

7*

York.   Mr. Emmett had travelled with circuses,
and had heard the performers refer to the States
south of Mason and Dixon's line as "Dixie's land,"
wishing themselves there as soon as the Northern
climate began to be too severe for those who live
in tents like the Arabs.   It was on this expression
of Northern circus performers,

I wish I was in Dixie,

that Mr. Emmett constructed his song.   The
"walk-around" hit the taste of the New-York play-
going public, and it was adopted at once by various
bands of wandering minstrels, who sang and danced
it in all parts of the Union.   In the fall of 1860
Mrs. John Wood sang it in New Orleans in John
Brougham's burlesque of 'Pocahontas,' and in
New Orleans it took root.   Without any authority
from the composer, a New Orleans publisher had
the air harmonized and arranged, and he issued it
with words embodying the strong Southern feeling of the chief city of Louisiana.   As from Boston
'John Brown's Body' spread through the North,
so from New Orleans 'Dixie' spread through the
South ; and as Northern poets strove to find fit
words for the one, so Southern poets wrote fiery
lines to fill the measures of the other.   Of the sets
of verse written to 'Dixie,' the best, perhaps, is

that by General Albert Pike, of Arkansas, who happens, by a fortuitous chance, to have been a native of Vermont. With Republican words 'Dixie' had been used as a campaign song in 1860; and it was perhaps some vague remembrance of this which prompted Lincoln to have the air played by a band in Washington in 1865, a short time after the surrender at Appomattox, remarking that as we had captured the rebel army we had captured also the rebel tune.

From New Orleans also came another of the songs of the South, the 'Bonnie Blue Flag.' Mr. Randall writes me that 'Dixie' and the 'Bonnie Blue Flag' were the most popular of Southern songs. Like 'Dixie,' the 'Bonnie Blue Flag' came from the theatre. The tune is an old Hibernian melody, the 'Irish Jaunting Car.' The earliest words were written by an Irish comedian, Harry McCarthy, and the song was first sung by his sister, Miss Marion McCarthy, at the Varieties Theatre, in 1861. It was published by Mr. A. E. Blackmar, who wrote to a friend of mine that General Butler " made it very profitable by fining every man, woman, or child who sang, whistled, or played it on any instrument, $25," besides arresting the publisher, destroying the sheet music, and fining him $500. Later a stirring lyric, to be sung to this air, was written by Miss Annie Chambers Ketcham.

In Louisiana, of course, there was also the 'Marseillaise.' "The Creoles of New Orleans," Mr. Cable has written me, "followed close by the Anglo-Americans of their town, took up the 'Marseillaise' with great enthusiasm, as they have always done whenever a war spirit was up. They did it when the British invaded Louisiana in 1814. It was good enough as it stood; they made no new adaptations of it, but sang it in French and English (I speak of 1861), 'dry so,' as the Southern rustics say. 'Dixie' started with the first mutter of war thunder. . . . I think the same is true of 'Lorena.' This doleful old ditty started at the start, and never stopped till the last musket was stacked and the last camp-fire cold. It was, by all odds, the song nearest the Confederate soldier's heart. It was the 'Annie Laurie' of the Confederate trenches."

Nowadays it is not a little difficult to detect in the rather mushy sentimentality of the words of 'Lorena,' or in the lugubrious wail of its music, any qualities which might account for the affection it was held in. But the vagaries of popular taste are inscrutable. Dr. Palmer's vigorous lyric, 'Stonewall Jackson's Way,' written within sound of the

cannonading at Antietam, was so little sung that
Mr. Randall thought it had not been set to music.
I have, however, succeeded in discovering two airs
to which it was sung—one published by Mr. Blackmar, and the other the familiar 'Duda, duda, day.'

The Northern equivalent of 'Lorena' is to be
sought among the songs which made a lyric address
to 'Mother,' and of which 'Just before the Battle,
Mother,' may be taken as a type.   'Mother, I've
Come Home to Die' was sung with feeling and
with humor by many a gallant fellow who is now
gathered at the bivouac of the dead.   Mr. George
F. Root, of Chicago, was both the author and composer of 'Just before the Battle, Mother,' as he was
also of the 'Battle Cry of Freedom,' and of 'Tramp,
Tramp, Tramp; the Boys are Marching.'   It is
difficult to say which one of these three songs was
the most popular; there was a touch of realistic
pathos in 'Just before the Battle, Mother,' which
brought the simple and unpretending words home
to the hearts of the men who had girded on the
sword and shouldered the musket.   Yet captivity
was not seldom more bitter to bear than death itself, and this gave point to the lament of the soldier
who sat in his "prison cell" and heard the tramp,
tramp, tramp of the marching boys.   Probably,
however, the first favorite with the soldiers in the

field, and certainly the song of Mr. Root's which has the best chance of surviving, is the 'Battle Cry of Freedom.' It was often ordered to be sung as the men marched into action. More than once its strains arose on the battle-field and made obedience more easy to the lyric command to rally round the flag. With the pleasant humor which never deserts the American, even in the hard tussle of war, the gentle lines of 'Mary had a Little Lamb' were fitted snugly to the tune; and many a regiment shortened a weary march or went gayly into action, singing,

> Mary had a little lamb,
> Its fleece was white as snow,
> Shouting the battle-cry of freedom;
> And everywhere that Mary went
> The lamb was sure to go,
> Shouting the battle-cry of freedom.

Now the song is sure of immortality, for it has become a part of those elective studies which are the chief gains of the college curriculum. At the hands of the American college boys, 'Rally round the Flag' can get a renewed lease of life for twenty-one years more—or forever. A boy is your true conservative; he is the genuine guardian of ancient rites and customs, old rhymes and songs; he has the fullest reverence for age—if so be it is not incarnated in a Prof. or the Prex.

Lowell, in declaring the antiquity of the New World, says that " we have also in America things amazingly old, as our boys, for example." And the borrowing of the ' Battle Cry of Freedom ' by the colleges is only the fair exchange which is no robbery; for, as we have seen, it was from the college that the air of ' Lauriger Horatius ' was taken to speed the heated stanzas of ' My Maryland.' Another college song,—if the digression may be pardoned,—the ' Upidee-Upida,' to which we so wickedly sing the quatrains of Longfellow's ' Excelsior,' I have heard rising sonorously from the throats of a stalwart regiment of German *Landwehr* in the summer of 1870, as they were on their way to the French frontier — and to Paris.

Although they came at the beginning of the war, ' John Brown's Body ' and the ' Battle Cry of Freedom ' have been sung scarcely more often than ' Marching through Georgia,' which could not have come into being until near the end of the fight. Now that the war has been over for twenty years and more, and the veteran has no military duty more harassing than fighting his battles o'er, ' Marching through Georgia ' has become the song dearest to his heart. The swinging rhythm of the tune and the homely directness of the words gave the song an instant popularity, increased by the

fact that it commemorated the most striking episode of the war, the march to the sea. 'Marching
through Georgia' was written and composed by
the late Henry C. Work. In his history of 'Music
in America,' Professor Ritter refers to Stephen C.
Foster, the composer of 'Old Folks at Home,' as one
who " said naïvely and gently what he had to say,
without false pretension or bombastic phrases";
and this praise may be applied also to Work, who
had not a little of the folk-flavor which gives quality
to Foster. Like Foster, Work was fond of reflect-
ing the rude negro rhythms; and some of his best
songs seem like actual echoes from the cotton-
field and levee. 'Wake, Nicodemus,' 'Kingdom
Coming,' and 'Babylon is Fallen' have this savor
of the soil,— sophisticated, it may be, and yet pun-
gent and captivating. I have heard it suggested
that 'Marching through Georgia' was founded
on a negro air, and also that it is a reminiscence
of a bit of the 'Rataplan' of the 'Huguenots.' It
is possible that there is a little truth at the bottom
of both of these stories. The 'Huguenots' was
frequently performed at the New Orleans Opera
House before the war, and many a slave must
have heard his young mistress singing and playing
selections from Meyerbeer's music; and it may be
that Work, in turn, overheard some negro's ram-

bling recollection of the 'Rataplan.' This is idle conjecture, however; the tune of 'Marching through Georgia' is fresh and spirited; and it bids fair—with 'John Brown's Body'—to be the chief legacy of the war. Work was also the author and composer of two other songs which had their day, 'Drafted into the Army' and 'Brave Boys are They.' The latter has had the honor of being sung of late by Mr. Cable, who heard first at a Southern camp-fire from the lips of a comrade the chorus of Northern origin, equally apt in its application in those troublous times to the homes on either side of Mason and Dixon's line:

> Brave boys are they,
>   Gone at their country's call;
> And yet — and yet we cannot forget
>   That many brave boys must fall.

It was in the dark days of 1862, just after Lincoln had issued the proclamation asking for three hundred thousand volunteers to fill up the stricken ranks of the army and to carry out the cry which urged it 'On to Richmond,' that Mr. John S. Gibbons wrote

> We are coming, Father Abraham,
>   Three hundred thousand more,

a lyric which contributed not a little to the bringing about of the uprising it declared. The author of this ringing call to arms was a member of the Society of Friends,—in other words, a Hicksite Quaker,—"with a reasonable leaning, however, toward wrath in cases of emergency," as his son-in-law, Mr. James H. Morse, neatly put it, in a recent letter to me. He joined the abolition movement in 1830, when he was barely twenty years old. Three years later he married a daughter of Isaac T. Hopper, the Quaker philanthropist. For a short time he was one of the editors of the *Anti-Slavery Standard*, and like many of the Quakers of his school, he was always ardent in the cause of negro freedom. At the outbreak of the war, Mrs. Gibbons and her eldest daughter went to the front, and they served in the hospitals until the end. While they were away the riots of '63 occurred, and their house in New-York was sacked, Mr. Gibbons and the two younger daughters taking refuge with relatives in the house next door but one, and thence over the roofs to Eighth Avenue, where Mr. Joseph H. Choate had a carriage in waiting for them. The house was singled out for this attention because it had been illuminated when the Emancipation Proclamation was issued,—on which occasion it had been daubed and defiled with coal tar.

At the request of Mr. Morse, Mr. Gibbons has put on paper an account of the circumstances under which he wrote 'We are coming, Father Abraham,' and from this I am privileged to quote. It must be premised that Mr. Gibbons, although he had written verse,—as who has not?—was best known as a writer on economic topics : he has published two books about banking and he was for a while the financial editor of the *Evening Post*.   In 1862, after Lincoln had issued his call for volunteers, Mr. Gibbons used to take long walks alone, often talking to himself. "I began to con over a song," he writes.   "The words seemed to fall into ranks and files, and to come with a measured step.   Directly would come along a company of soldiers with fife and drum, and that helped the matter amazingly.   I began to keep step myself—three hun-dred thousand more.   It was very natural to answer the President's call—we are coming—and to prefix the term *father*.   Then the line would follow.

We are coming, Father Abraham,

and nothing was more natural than the number of soldiers wanted.

Three hundred thousand more.
We are coming, Father Abraham, three hundred thousand
more.

" Where from ?   *Shore* is the rhyme wanted."
Just then Mr. Gibbons met " a western regiment—from Minnesota, it was—and the line
came at once in full,

> From Mississippi's winding stream, and from New Eng-
> land's shore.

" Two lines in full . . . Then followed—how
naturally !

> We leave our ploughs and workshops, our wives and children
> dear,
> With hearts too full for utterance, with but a silent tear.

" And so it went on, word by word, line by
line, until the whole song was made."   When it
was written, only one slight verbal alteration was
made, and then it was printed in the *Evening Post*
of July 16, 1862.   It is interesting to note that it
was in the *Evening Post* of May 29, 1819, nearly
half a century before, that another famous patriotic
poem had first been published—Drake's ' American Flag.'   Mr. Gibbons's song appeared anonymously and its authorship was ascribed at once to
Bryant, who was then the editor of the *Evening
Post*.   At a large meeting in Boston, held the
evening after it had appeared, it was read by Josiah
Quincy as " the latest poem written by Mr. Wm.
C. Bryant."

One of the Hutchinson family set it to music, and they sang it with great effect. A common friend told Jesse Hutchinson that the song was not by Bryant but by Mr. Gibbons. "What—our old friend Gibbons?" he asked in reply. It is reported that when he was assured that his old friend Gibbons was the real author of the song, Jesse Hutchinson hesitated thoughtfully for a moment and then said, "Well, we'll keep the name of Bryant, as we've got it. He's better known than Gibbons." The stirring song was set to music by several other composers, most of whom probably supposed that it was Bryant's. I find in a stray newspaper cutting an account of Lincoln's coming down to the Red Room of the White House one morning in the summer of 1864, to listen with bowed head and patient, pensive eyes while one of a party of visitors sang

We are coming, Father Abraham, three hundred thousand
    more.

A rattling good war song which has kept its hold on the ears of the people is 'When Johnny comes Marching Home,' published in 1863 by "Louis Lambert." Behind this pseudonym was hidden Mr. P. S. Gilmore, the projector of the Boston "Peace Jubilee," and the composer afterward of a more ambitious national hymn, which has hitherto failed to attain the popularity of its unpretending predecessor with the rousing refrain. It is related that after the performance of 'Glory to God on High,' from Mozart's Twelfth Mass, on the first day of the Jubilee, an old soldier of the Webster regiment took occasion to shake hands with Mr. Gilmore and to proffer his congratulations on the success of the undertaking, adding that for his part what he had liked best was the piece called the ' Twelfth Massachusetts.'

At the Boston Peace Jubilee, and again at the Centennial Exhibition, there was opportunity for the adequate and serious treatment of the war tunes which have survived the welter and turmoil of the actual struggle ; but the occasion was not improved.   Little more has been done than a chance arrangement of airs in the clap-trap manner of Jullien's ' British Army Quadrilles.'   The ' Centennial March ' which Richard Wagner wrote for us was the work of a master, no doubt, but it was perfunctory, and hopelessly inferior to his resplendent ' Kaiser March.'   The German composer had not touch of the American people, and as he did not know what was in our hearts, we had no right to hope that he should give it expression.   The time is now ripe for the musician who shall richly and

amply develop with sustained and sonorous dignity the few simple airs which represent and
recall to the people of these United States the
emotions, the doubts, the dangers, the joys, the
sorrows, the harassing anxieties, and the final
triumph of the four long years of bitter strife. The
composer who will take 'John Brown's Body'
and 'Marching through Georgia,' and such other
of our war tunes as may be found worthy, and
who shall do unto them as the still living Hunga-
rian and Scandinavian composers have done to
the folk-songs of their native land, need not hesi-
tate from poverty of material or from fear of the
lack of a responsive audience. The first American
composer who shall turn these war tunes into
mighty music to commemorate the events which
called them forth, will of a certainty have his reward.

ON THE FRENCH SPOKEN BY THOSE WHO DO NOT SPEAK FRENCH.

I HAVE always thought it a great pity that Thackeray did not leave us a Roundabout Paper ' On the French spoken by those who do not speak French.' No one is so competent and so capable of doing justice to the topic as Thackeray. It is a subject which seems most suitable for the author of the ' Book of Snobs '; for, above all things, is there snobbishness in the affectation of being on speaking terms with the French language, when in very truth it barely returns your bow. The title of the proposed paper is perhaps a little long ; but there is wealth enough of material to warrant an article as ample as the name may promise. Indeed, the title is almost too comprehensive, for it includes the blunders of those who know they cannot speak French, but nevertheless try to make themselves understood, and the errors of those who insist in thinking that they can speak French in spite of oral testimony which convinces every one else. And it would also include certain extraordinary phrases which pass for French in ordinary English speech.

The first of these classes is the French of Stratford-at-Bow, the French of the Hoosier or the Cockney, the French of those who affectionately refer to the capital of France as " Parry "— as though it were an Arctic explorer ; there are even those, I am told, who descend so low as " Parree," because, mayhap, like *Mrs. General Gilflory,* they " have been so long abroad." At this type the French themselves never tire of poking fun. In caricature, pictorial or dramatic, it is an endless source of amusement; and the seeker for illustrative anecdote has an abundance to choose from. One of the most amusing is a dialogue between a Cockney passenger, who has full belief in the purity of his French, and the conductor of a diligence. The Cockney begins by calling the coachman a pig — and, indeed, *cocher* is not so very unlike *cochon.* Then he addresses himself to the conductor :

" Etes-vous le diligence ? "

" Non, m'sieur, je suis le conducteur."

" C'est tout le même chose. Donnez-moa doux places dans votre interieur."

8

Unable tó get inside seats, he tries to mount to the roof.   Unfortunately, he slips and falls heavily to the ground.   The conductor runs to his assistance.

" Avez-vous de mal, m'sieur ? "

" No, moa pas de malle, moa only a portmanteau."

Here the blunderer was English ; but in another narrative it seems to me that the fault lies rather with the Frenchman.   An Anglo-Saxon was travelling in the south of France, and once, as the train into the station drew, he asked an attendant :

" Est-ce que c'est içi Hyères ? "

Unfortunately, he pronounced the name of the town as though it were written *hier ;* and so he received the puzzled answer :

" Mais non, m'sieur, c'est içi aujourd'hui."

Of honest blundering in the use of the foreign tongue, and of frank ignorance, there is no lack of anecdotes.   The young lady brought up in an establishment where "French is the language of the school " is not always above asking " qu'elle est la matière ? " and telling you that " il n'y a pas de dépêche," when she means to inquire what may be the matter, and to inform you that there is no hurry.   I believe that Americans pick up French more quickly than do the English ; but when one seeks for typical blunders of beginners and of pretenders, honors are easy. It was a young American who asked for "*café au lait* without any milk," and who alluded to "*gendre* pictures," and who described a dress as "trimmed all down the front with *bouillon* fringe." But internal evidence compels me to assign to an Englishman the part of the protagonist in two merry jests of this sort. In one he says, "Je veux un poitrine de caleçons," and it is discovered that he had dug out from the dictionary this translation of "chest of drawers.' In the other the scene is laid on a channel steamer, and as this thrusts its nose into the chopping sea, an English bagman calls frantically for the steward, adding, "Je sens mauvais. Où est ma naissance?" I have been told that he supposed he was saying the French equivalent for "I feel bad. Where is my berth?"

An American again, and a rigid Republican, is the hero of another anecdote. He met the German king who has won fame in the study of Dante, and he told his majesty that he was pleased to meet him. He parted from the royal scholar with the remark, "Je vous honore pas comme roi mais comme écolier!" It is a strange sight to see two Anglo-Saxon strangers meet and "terrify each other into mutual unintelligibility with that *lingua*

franca of the English-speaking traveller, which is
supposed to bear some remote affinity to the French
language, of which both parties are as ignorant as
an American ambassador "— as Mr. Lowell wrote
in his 'Fireside Travels,' not foreseeing the time
when the scholar in politics should be minister at
Madrid and London.

When Dr. Holmes acted as a medium and mate-
rialized the sturdy spectre of Dr. Johnson, the earlier autocrat declared to the later that "to trifle
with the vocabulary, which is the vehicle of social
intercourse, is to tamper with the currency of
human intelligence"; and the orotund presence
added the characteristic sentiment that in his
opinion "he who would violate the sanctities of
his mother-tongue would invade the recesses of
the paternal till without remorse, and repeat the
banquet of Saturn without indigestion." From
the context we learn that just then the spirit of the
great lexicographer had been perturbed by certain
trifling puns or verbal witticisms with which the
breakfast-table had been amused ; but his ponder-
ous criticism has always seemed to me to be quite
as applicable to the ill-advised speakers and writers
who find the English language inadequate to the
full expression of their teeming thoughts, and who
are therefore forced to filch phrases from foreign
tongues.

The habit of dropping into French, for example, is as enfeebling as the habit of punning ; and the one is quite as fairly to be considered a violation of the sanctities of the mother-tongue as the other. Either habit indicates a certain flabbiness of fibre, intellectual as well as ethical. It is difficult to believe either in the moral rectitude or in the mental strength of a man or of a woman addicted to the quoting of odd scraps of odd French. When we take up the latest work of a young-lady-novelist, and when we find scattered through her pages *soubriquet*, and *double-entendre*, and *nom de plume*, and *à l'outrance*, and other words and phrases which no Frenchman knows, we need not read further to be sure that the mantle of Jane Austen and George Eliot has not fallen on the shoulders of the fair author. Even Mrs. Oliphant, a novelist who is old enough to know better, and who has delighted us all with her charming tales of truly English life, is wont to sprinkle French freely through her many volumes, not in her novels only, but even in her unnecessary memoir of Sheridan, whom she credits with *gaité du cœur*. In his 'Letter to Young Contributors,' Colonel Higginson gave sound advice to the literary tyro when suggesting that he should "avoid French as some of the fashionable novelists avoid English."

Has any one ever noted that there is a far greater fondness in England for French words and phrases than there is in America? Whether I am the discoverer or not, the fact seems to me to be beyond question. In the new Grand Hotel in London, which is supposed to be managed on the American plan, more or less, but which has a name borrowed from Paris, the very gorgeous dining-room is labeled *Salle à Manger*. In another English hotel I saw a sign on what we call the " elevator," and the English, with greater simplicity, term a " lift," declaring it to be an *ascenseur*. The portable fire-extinguisher familiar to all Americans as a " Babcock," is in England called an *extincteur*. On the programmes of the itinerant opera company managed by Mr. Mapleson, and called, comically enough, Her Majesty's Opera, the wig-maker and costumer appear as the *perruquier* and the *costumier*. In the window of a shop in Regent Street, toward the end of the season, I saw exposed for sale a handsome china tea-service in a handsome silk-lined box, bearing in its cover two little placards, that to the right declaring that it was suitable for A Wedding Present, while that on the left suggested its fitness as *Un Présent De Noces*. In another English shop I have seen a heap of napkins surmounted by a placard setting forth the

price of these *serviettes*, and not far off was a pile
of oddly named *serviette*-rings. But perhaps this
is not more painful than a sign still to be seen in
New Bond Street, declaring that the house to which
it is affixed is occupied by " Blank et Cie., Artistes
in Corsets." This, in the language of the wild
Western humorist after he had been to Paris, *frappe
tout chose parfaitement froid!*

Of course it cannot be denied that certain French
words (and not those only which came over with
the Conqueror) have fairly won a right of domicile
in England. *Ennui*, for example, and *pique*—these
have no exact English equivalents, and their re-
moval from common speech would leave an aching
void. (To *dénouement* I shall recur later.) But
why should we speak of an *employé* when the
regularly formed "employee" is at our service?
And what evil spirit possesses Mrs. Tompkins, the
London milliner, and Miss Simkins, the London
dressmaker, to emblazon their golden signs with
the mystic "Mdme. Tompkins, Modes," and
"Mdlle. Simkins, Robes"? And here occasion
serves to protest, with whatever strength may in
me lie, against the superfluous *d* which British custom has injected into the French contractions for
Madame and *Mademoiselle*. We say British, for
this error is confined to Great Britain and her co-

lonial dependencies, the inhabitants of the United States of America having happily escaped it. In America, as in France, *Madame* and *Mademoiselle* are contracted to *Mme.* and *Mlle.*, and it is only the Briton who writes *Mdme.* and *Mdlle.*, in the fond belief that he has caught the exact Parisian touch. I venture to hint also that even after a French word has been admitted into the English language, the Englishman is inclined to recall its foreign origin in pronouncing it, while the American treats it frankly as an English word. Thus *charade* has nearly the same sound in the mouth of an educated Englishman that it has in the mouth of a Frenchman, whereas it falls from the lips of an American as a perfect rhyme for "made." And in like manner *trait* retains its French pronunciation in Great Britain, while in the United States it is spoken as it is spelt — to rhyme with "strait." The pun in the title of Dr. Doran's 'Table Traits, with something on them,' wholly evades an American unfamiliar with the British usage. But the American who girds at this English peculiarity must remember that he has heard his fellow-citizens call a *menu* a "maynew," and a *début* a "debyou"; and that some of them are in doubt whether *dépôt* ought to rhyme happily with "Aleppo," or haply with "teapot," and there-

fore compromise illogically by rhyming it with
" sweep oh ! "

To the ignorant and affected misuse of French
or quasi-French, there is another kind of snobbishness closely akin and deserving castigation as
severe. It is the use of the native name of a place,
or worse yet, of the French name, instead of the
English.   What sort of figure would be cut by a
returned traveller who described his journeys and
his sojournings in *Italia* and *Deutschland?*   Is it
not as bad to speak of Mainz? and worse still, of
Mayence?— when there is an honest English name,
Mentz, inscribed in a hundred lusty chronicles of
illustrious wars?   And how often do we hear
ladies talk of Malines lace, meaning the while the
lace made at Mechlin,— for the town is Dutch,
although the French have chosen to give it a name
of their own fashioning, as they have also to Mentz
and many another city.

It may be as well to note that the French phrase
is *à outrance,* that there is no *u* in *sobriquet,* and
that the French know no such expression as *nom de
plume* or *double-entendre,* the nearest approach to
the one being *nom de guerre* and to the other *double entente,* a double meaning, which is, however,
wholly devoid of the ulterior significance attached
to *double-entendre.* Perhaps the word most sinned

8*

against is *artiste*. There is really no excuse whatever for the use of this word in English speech.
It is the exact translation and complete equivalent
of the English word *artist,* and it does not mean
a female artist any more than *pianiste* means a
female pianist. I can now recall with a shudder
a programme thrust into my hand at a watering-
place two or three years ago, in which a certain
charming artist was announced as " the greatest
living lady pianiste in the world." *Encore,* although
used in English in a sense wholly different from
that which it has in French, has now taken out its
naturalization papers ; and so has a hybrid word
parquette used in America to indicate what the
English call the stalls or orchestra chairs.

But on the stage, or rather in writings for and
of and about the stage, there is an enormous con-
sumption of French phrases, or of phrases fondly
supposed to be French. The dramatic critic is wont
to refer to the *rentrée* of an old favorite when he
means his or her reappearance ; and he comments
on the skilful way in which M. Sardou brings
about his *dénoûment,*— and for this there is perhaps some excuse, as there is no English word
which is the exact technical equivalent of dénoûment. But he will record the attempting of a new
rôle by the *ingénue,* and he will congratulate that

clever *comédienne* on the enlarging of her *repertoire*. To him the " juvenile lead " is a *jeune premier* and the tragic actress is a *tragédienne* educated at the *conservatoire*. In his eyes a ballet-dancer is a *danseuse,* and in his ears the comic singer sings a *chansonnette*. There is really no reason for this frequent French ; and although the vocabulary of the dramatic critic is overworked, with a little care he may avoid tautology by less violent means.

Over the door of a free-and-easy or cheap concert-saloon near Union Square I have seen a transparency announcing that the place was a " Resorté Musicale." And in a theatrical weekly paper I discovered once an advertisement even more remarkable. I give it here as it stood, changing only the proper names :

ANNIE BLACK,

The popular favorite and Leading Lady of —— Theatre Comique, will be at liberty after June to engage for the season of '81-82, as Leading Lady with first-class comb. Also

E. J. BLACK,

(*Née* EDWARD BROWN,)

CHARACTER ACTOR.

Please read this carefully, and note the delightfully inappropriate use of *née,* and the purely professional cutting short into " comb." of the word

"combination," technically applied to strolling
companies.   Above all, pray remark the fact that
the gray mare is the better horse, and that the man
has given up his own name for his wife's.

It would not be fair thus to rebuke our fellow-
countrymen without noting the fact that the French
are nowadays quite as prone to quote English as
the English are to quote French, and also that there
is very little to choose between the results.   An
article on sport in a French paper is almost as curious and macaronic a medley as an article on the
fashions in an English paper.   Just as the technical phrases which hint at the mighty mysteries
of ladies' apparel are all French, so the technical
phrases of masculine outdoor amusement are nearly
all English.   The report of a horse-race as it appears in a Parisian newspaper is quite as comic as
the description of a bride's gown as it appears in
a London organ of society.   The French dandy,
who was once a *gandin,* and who is now a *gom-
meux,* is driven to the course in a *breach* drawn by
a pair of *steppers;* on the track he mingles with
the *betting-men* and makes a *book.*   Thus he ac-
complishes his duty to society, and is acknowledged to be *tout ce qu'il y a de plus high-lif.*   We
are informed and believe that this strange perversion of "high life" is pronounced as it is written,

" hig-lif." When the French swell is not mingling with the other *sportmen* on the *turf,* he has perhaps gone to the river to see the *rovingmen,* or into some garden to watch the *jeunes misses* playing *crockett,* by which last word the French are wont to designate the formerly popular game of croquet. In the summer, or rather in the early autumn, he varies these amusements by a paperchase of some unknown variety, which he complacently calls a *rallye-papier.*

To see just how far can go this absurd commingling of tongues, complicated by preternaturally ingenious blundering, one must give his days and nights to the reading of the 'Carnet d'un Mondain,' which the *Figaro* publishes under the signature of " Etincelle." To see how even clever and well-informed writers may err in bad company, one must read the always interesting and often instructive *chroniques* which M. Jules Claretie contributed every week to the *Temps,* and which were gathered together every year under the title of 'La Vie à Paris.' M. Claretie reads English, and he has travelled in England; but he makes repeated use of a hybrid verb —*interwiever,* which we assume to be some sort of a Gallicized interview. *Interwiever* is the act accomplished by the *reporter*—another word which the French have snatched across the Channel. But *interwiever,* bad as it is, and absurd as it is, is not a whit worse or more absurd than *double-entendre* and *soubriquet.* In fact, the better one knows the popular misinformation on both sides of the Channel, the more willingly will one admit that honors are easy, and that English bad French is no better and no worse than French bad English.

Ten years ago M. Justin Amero put forth two little pamphlets full of the most amusing blunders of the Anglo-Frenchman and the Franco-Englishman. One, 'L'Anglomanie dans le français et les barbarismes anglais usités en France,' was intended to warn those of his fellow-countrymen who write "Times is money" in the belief that they are quoting Shakspere; and the other, 'French Gibberish,' a review showing how the French language is misused in England and in other English-speaking countries, was meant for those who write *coute qui coute* instead of *coute que coute.*

There is an ancient and musty jest about a city madam who spoke only the French habitually used in young ladies' schools, and who rendered into English the familiar *ris de veau à la financière* as "a smile of the little cow in the manner of the female financier." But this is not more startling than many other things to be discovered by those

who search the cook-books diligently. I remember a bill of fare in an American hotel in which
all the familiar dishes were translated into unfamiliar French, the climax being reached when ginger-
snaps, the sole dessert, appeared transmogrified into
gateux de gingembre.   Perhaps it is in revenge for
repeated insults like this that the Parisians now
advertise on the windows of the cafés on the boule-
vards that *Boissons Américaines* are sold within,
the only American drink particularized being a certain " Shery Gobbler," warranted to warm the
heart of all vagrant American humorists who may
chance to visit Paris while alive and in the flesh.
In essence *shery gobbler* is but little more comic
than *rosbif*, or than *bifteck*, which are recognized
French forms of the roast beef of old England and
of the beefsteak which plays second to it.   Both
rosbif and *bifteck* are accepted by Littré, who finds
for the latter a sponsor as early and as eminent as
Voltaire.   And *shery gobbler* is not as comic as "cutlete" and " tartlete," which I detected day after
day on the bill of fare of a Cunard steamer crossing
from Liverpool to New-York three or four years
ago.   When I drew the attention of a fellow-
traveller to the constant recurrence of the superfluous *e* at the end of cutlet and tartlet, the active and
intelligent steward, who anticipated our slightest

wants, leant forward with a benignant smile, and
benevolently explained the mystery. "It's the
French, sir," he said; "cutlete and tartlete is
French, sir!"

A bill of fare at the Grand Hotel in Paris, in
1885, offered "Irisch-stew à la française"—truly
a marvellous dish.   In a certain restaurant of the
Palais Royal, however, there is a bi-lingual bill of
fare which recalls the Portuguese 'Guide to Conversation,' if indeed it does not "break the record."
In this we are proffered our choice of "barbue
dutch manner" *(barbue à la Hollandaise),* or "eel
in tartar," or of "a sole at Colbert." We may
have "beef at flamande" or "beef at mode" *(bœuf
à la mode),* or "beefsteack with haricots." The
cotelette sauté à la minute appears as "one mutton
chop at minute," and a *cotelette de chevreuil* appears
as "a chops of kid" *(sic).* We may order, if we
will, a "fillet napolitan manner," or a "chicken at
Marengo," or a "sweet bread at financière."

But quite the wildest linguistic freak which ever
came within my ken is the following notice, copied
years ago from the original as it hung on the walls
of a cheap hotel in New-York frequented by the
smaller theatrical people of all nationalities : "Mes-
sier et Médammes chaque Diners, soupés, etc., se
que ont portez dan le chambres son chargait â par."

Of the many amusing stories in circulation and turning on an English misuse of French, the most popular is perhaps the anecdote in which one of two gentlemen occupying an apartment in Paris leaves word with the *concierge* that he does not wish his fire to go out; as he unfortunately expresses this desire in the phrase "ne laissez pas sortir le fou," much inconvenience results to the other gentleman, who is detained in the apartment as a dangerous lunatic. This pleasant tale has in its time been fathered on many famous Englishmen. And like unto it is another which Americans are wont to place to the credit of a Cockney, while the English are sure that its true hero was a Yankee—both parties acting on the old principle of "putting the Frenchman up the chimney when the tale is told in England." The story goes that a certain Anglo-Saxon—for thus I may avoid international complications—entered into a Parisian restaurant with intent to eat, drink, and be merry. Wishing to inform the waiter of his hunger he said, "J'ai une femme!" to which the polite but astonished waiter naturally responded, "J'espère que madame se porte bien?" Whereupon the Anglo-Saxon makes a second attempt at the French for hunger, and asserts, "Je suis fameux!" to which the waiter's obvious reply is,

"Je suis bien aise de le savoir, monsieur!" Then the Anglo-Saxon girded up his loins and made a final effort, and declared, "Je suis femme!" to which the waiter could answer only, "Alors madame s'habille d'une façon très-étrange." After which the Anglo-Saxon fled and was seen no more. This merry jest came to me by word of mouth and vouched for by an eye-witness; but I am told on good authority that it was used by the elder Charles Mathews in one of his At Homes at least half a century ago.

POKER-TALK.

E are "the Romans of the modern world—the great assimilating people." So the autocrat of all the Americas has declared, proving his case by offering in evidence our army sword which "is the short, stiff, pointed gladium of the Romans; and the American bowie-knife is the same tool, modified to meet the daily wants of civil society." In the armory of the Tower of London, the attendant used to show a curiously complicated and many-barreled pistol, and he was wont to remark that the American, Colonel Colt, "examined that there pistol very carefully, sir," and that "not long after he went and invented Colt's revolver, sir." So it is always; the steamboat and the turret-ship, the sewing machine and the mowing machine, the telegraph and the telephone, all inventions whereon an American may pride himself, are claimed by others; even the

six-shooter of Colonel Colt was invented by Queen
Elizabeth, and the Arkansas toothpick is nothing
more than the Roman broadsword. So it is
especially with all games ; the Canadian Lacrosse
may have come from the Indians ; but the more
national Base-ball is but the British Rounders—
amplified and beautified, it is true. One may
assert as an incontrovertible axiom that no game
is ever invented. Nowadays, at least, the human
mind is unequal to the making of a new one ; a
novel sport is always evolved from some other and
older game, and never from the inner consciousness of man. Even those highly characteristic
products of American ingenuity, facile Euchre and
fascinating Poker, are not truly American inventions ; they are at most but skilful modifications
or adaptations of earlier games. I know that
when you rob the American of the revolver and
the bowie-knife, when you strip the American
Eagle of both Euchre and Poker, you leave him
naked indeed ; but the truth must prevail.

The game of Euchre is first cousin to the game
of Écarté ; probably both are derived remotely from
the game of Triomphe or French Ruff. Cavendish
says that the French settlers in America took Triomphe with them and transformed it into Euchre.
This assertion seems hasty and sweeping, but

Euchre has prevailed more particularly along the Mississippi River, and it may have been acclimated there by some Canadian voyageur.

Euchre is not necessarily derived from either Écarté or Triomphe, despite the obvious similarity. The dog and the wolf are strangely alike, and so are the rose and the cabbage; and in time, perhaps both Écarté and Euchre may be traced back to the same germ or rudimentary game, from which it will be shown that they have been slowly evolved, differentiating themselves in accord with their environments. There is a precision and a logic about the Parisian Écarté which is wanting in the Euchre of the Mississippi, while the latter has a license and a rapidity suited to the recreative needs of the hardworking people of "a country where," as Mr. Lowell puts it, "the nomad population carry no household gods with them but their five wits and their ten fingers." The chief peculiarity of the game of Euchre is that it legalizes the dethroning of the upstart ace and the legitimate king and the usurpation of the supreme place by the wily jack; and that this usurpation is aided and abetted by the other jack of the same color. It is told that when the father of a family lay dying in a little river town of Kentucky he called his sons to his bedside that he might give a few words of solemn

advice for their future guidance in life. "Boys,"
he said, raising himself on one elbow, and no
doubt recalling a bitter memory of his own youth,
"when you go down the river to Orleens jest you
beware of a game called Yucker, where the jack
takes the ace;—it's unchristian!" And with this
final warning he lay back on his bed and died
in peace. I have always understood that it was
Euchre which the two gentlemen were playing on a
boat on the Missouri River when a by-stander,
shocked by the frequency with which one of the
players turned up the jack, took the liberty of warning the other player that the winner was dealing
from the bottom, to which the loser, secure in his
power of self-protection, answered gruffly, "Well,
suppose he is—it's his deal, isn't it?" It was,
perhaps, the playing of some remote progenitor
of Euchre that Shakspere had in mind when he
wrote—if I may risk a conjectural emendation and
substitute "knave" for "king" (obviously logical
and appropriate)—

> But while he thought to steal the single ten
> The *Knave* was slyly fingered from the deck.
>
> [Third part of 'King Henry VI.,' Act V., scene ii.]

"Deck" for "pack" is, of course, an Americanism; but Shakspere, who could not spell his own

name, may perhaps be forgiven for having dropped into an Americanism now and then.

The pedigree of Poker may be set forth with a little more certainty than we can declare the ancestry of Euchre. Mr. Jones—not quite so sound on Poker as he is on Whist—sees its origin in a game which the Italians of the Fifteenth Century called Il Frusso. During the next hundred years this had matured into Primiera, which was known in Spain as Primero and to Master Francis Rabelais in France as La Prime. It was closely akin to two other games which the French called Le Meslé and L'Ambigu, and to a third which the English knew as Gleek and the French as Le Glic— *cf.* Villon's 'Ballade de Bonne Doctrine à ceux de Mauvaise Vie':

> Gaigne au Berlan, au Glic, aux Quilles,
> Où s'en va tout, ou escoutez ;
> Tout au taverne et aux filles.

It crossed the channel to England, where it passed under a host of aliases, as might have been expected from a game of such doubtful antecedents. It was played as Primo, as Primero, as Gleek, and as Post-and-pair. Of course these games may have differed not a little in detail, but the vital principle was identical in all. Allusions to them

are abundant in the Elizabethan dramatists.   In
Ben Jonson's 'Every Man Out of His Humor' (Act
I., scene ii.), Carlo Buffone tells Sogliardo that "to
be an accomplished gentleman" he must "learn
to play Primero."   Falstaff confesses, "I have
never prospered since I forswore myself at Primero."   And in 'Every Man in His Humor' (Act
IV., scene ii.), Wellborn cries, "Here's a trick vied
and revied," as who should say, "Here's a bet,
seen and raised."

If we may rely on the testimony of the playmakers of the period—and the stage seems to
have reflected the manners of the time more
exactly under Elizabeth than it does now under
Victoria—we may fairly accept Gleek as the favorite pastime of the bold admirals who grappled
bravely with the mighty Armada, on the towering
ships of which the grandees of Spain were playing
Primero to beguile the time till they should sack
London.   And no doubt Post-and-pair pleased and
rejoiced the gentleman adventurer ranging the
Spanish Main during the next century, as its offspring, Poker, pleased and rejoiced the Argonauts
of '49, who, two hundred years and more thereafter, took possession of a distant possession
of the once magnificent realm of Spain.   The
younger band was as reckless as the elder, as de-

termined, as unhesitating, and it was fit that they
should recreate themselves with the same game—
a game, too, singularly suited to their characteristics and to their temperament, and calling for
courage, for insight, for shrewdness, and for a
prompt and certain knowledge of their fellow-
man.

In the course of years Primero seems to have
passed away and Gleek to have gone out of fashion, but Post-and-pair held its own. In 1674
Cotton wrote that "Five Cards is as much played
in Ireland as All Fours is in Kent and Post-and-pair
is in the west of England." Possibly it was from
the west of England that Post-and-pair went further "out west" in America and suffered a sea
change in the journey and became Brag. Now
Poker is the child of Brag, and Brag is the child of
Post-and-pair. "Poker (originally played in America) may be described as developed Brag, though
in some respects it 'throws back' to the parent
games Post-and-pair, L'Ambigu and Primero," so
Mr. Jones tells us, speaking as one having authority, in the latest edition of the 'Encyclopædia Britannica.' But of Poker there are, or rather, there
were, many kinds; and the first to develop was
Straight Poker. From Straight Poker came Draw
Poker, just as Short Whist came from Long Whist;

and when one says Poker nowadays he means thereby the more modern and scientific game of Draw Poker, just as when he says Whist he means the modern and scientific game of Short Whist. It was toward the end of the last century that "Short Whist started up and overthrew the Long Dynasty," so we are told by Major A., whose book on the subject has been edited by Professor P.; but it was not until after the Battle of Waterloo that the younger game finally vanquished the older. Many years later was it when Draw Poker succeeded in supplanting Straight Poker. Mr. Jefferson Davis, some time President of the late Confederate States of America, when charged with being too fond of the fascinating game while he was an officer of the United States Army at Prairie du Chien, in 1834, made answer and testified that Draw Poker had not been then introduced. So far as one may declare on the insufficient evidence now presented, Draw Poker came to the front early in the forties and was spread abroad during the war with Mexico and generally accepted as the true game of Poker, before the day when gold was most unexpectedly discovered in the California which Mexico had ceded to the United States at the signing of the peace, and to which there was at once an over-

whelming rush of the vigorous youth of America.
By selection and by cultivation a higher type of
game had been developed in the very nick of time,
at the precise psychologic moment when it was
needed for use by the energetic and quick-witted
throng of ardent young men who were about to
wrest vast wealth from the barren hills of the
State which had taken for its motto the happy cry
of Archimedes.   When once the myriad possibilities of Draw Poker, its manifold beauties and its
exact fitness for the work in hand began to be
perceived, its future was assured.   The fate of
Straight Poker was sealed irrevocably; there was
no hope for it, although it might linger for yet a while
in outlying corners of the country, as the Britons
tarried after the Saxon invasion and conquest.
Long before the breaking out of the Rebellion it
was evident that Draw Poker had come to stay
and that thereafter Straight Poker, with its ill-
named fellows, Stud Poker and Whisky Poker,
must sink to the level of poor relations, who must
content themselves, like Shakspere's widow, with
the second-best bed.

As one of the brightest jewels in Britannia's
crown is the inventing, or rather the perfecting, of
Whist, so the development of Poker is one of the
chief glories of Columbia.   The ancestry of Poker

has been declared above, and it may be well, therefore, to note that the lordly Whist was once known as the humble Swobbers. The new Whist, having reached the highest point of perfection, has been fixed and established by the final codification of its laws. The new Poker has not yet found its John Lorraine Baldwin to draw up its rules with the needful conciseness and certainty. It cannot be asserted that the laws of Poker lie hid in night, like those of Nature before Newton, and of Whist before Mr. Baldwin,—to use Mr. Hayward's happy figure,—but they are in darkness and in doubt. At present Poker may be said to be governed by the common law, ignorance whereof excuseth no man. Local usages vary; contradictory *obiter dicta* of self-constituted judges abound; and more than one important point remains undecided for want of a written text of the law and of an authorized tribunal. The supremacy of the Straight Flush has got itself slowly acknowledged at last. Whether or not Straights beat Threes is still a mooted point; the better opinion is that they do, and it is so held in the proposed code drawn up by the learned American once resident at the Court of St. James. There are those who do not recognize Straights at all; and there are others who admit the Mississippi obtrusion of Blazes. The accepted order of the hands at Poker was set forth a few years ago by my friend, the editor of *Puck*, in a mnemonic table of great international utility. The man of genius who drew it up was aware that every Englishman knew the proper precedence of the various orders of the nobility and gentry, and that every American knew the relative values of the various Poker hands. It will be seen, therefore, that while his invention indicates to the Cockney the hierarchy of the hands at Poker, it provides the Yankee with a table of precedence for use in Great Britain and her colonial dependencies:

IN GREAT BRITAIN.	IN THE UNITED STATES.
A Royal Duke	A Straight Flush
A Duke	Four of a kind
A Marquis	A Full
An Earl	A Flush
A Viscount	A Straight
A Baron	Three of a kind
A Baronet	Two Pairs
A Knight	One Pair

The invention of the Straight Flush (called a Royal Flush when it begins with the ace and ends with the ten) and the concession of its absolute precedence have removed an awkward stumbling-block from the path of the upright and punctilious Poker player. There are many possible Straight

Flushes and they may be inferior one to another ;
no Straight Flush, however imposing it may be in
appearance, is sure to win, like Tommy Dodd ;
even Mr. John Doe's combined ace, king, queen,
knave, and ten of diamonds may be equalled by Mr.
Richard Roe's united ace, king, queen, knave, and
ten of spades, and the stakes would not fall to
either but must needs be divided between both.
But if there were no Straight Flush, then Four
Aces would be absolute and invincible ; and he
who happily held Four Aces would know himself

Quite irresistible
Like a man with eight trumps in his hand at a whist-table.

Before the accession of the Royal Flush to the
imperial throne there was often heard an impossible opinion that as Four Aces was "a sure
thing," no gentleman would bet on them. If
this proposition had been universally accepted
Four Aces, as a hand, ceased to exist practically ;
and with this abdication of Four Aces, of course
Four Kings became "a sure thing" in their turn ;
and by an application of the same logic no gentleman would bet on them — which is absurd.

The Royal Flush is not often seen ; like other
exalted monarchs it does not make itself common
in men's eyes. I have played three and four

nights in succession without an audience with his
imperial majesty. I have rarely played without
the presence of Fours, two or three times at least
in the course of the evening. There are certain
lewd fellows of the baser sort who are given to
playing Poker with a short pack of thirty-two
cards used for Euchre, Écarté, and Piquet. The
altitude of the hands one can hold in rapid succession in this bastard sport is startling enough.
Three of a kind is as nothing, and a Flush is cut
down in the twinkling of an eye. It takes a little
while to get used to the change of the combinations in their relative importance. The greater
frequency of apparently gigantic hands leads many
Euchre players now and again to wish audibly that
they were playing Poker. It is well for them that
their wish is not granted. In the nursery tale the
wood-cutter and his wife, who had three wishes,
did not find them very profitable, and most of
those who express a desire to change for a moment from Euchre to Poker would find they had
jumped from the frying-pan into the fire.

There is the leading case of the commercial traveller in the Pullman car on the Pacific Railroad. He
had fraternized with a mining millionaire who
owed his fortune to his faculty of taking advantage of an opportunity and of his fellow-man.   As

the train sped across the prairie they dropped into
a friendly game of Euchre.   After they had played
for an hour or so, the millionaire dealt and turned
up a queen, and the eyes of the commercial traveller brightened as he gazed on his hand.

" I wish we were playing Poker," he ventured.

The mine owner looked over his cards and answered not.

" What do you say to changing the game?"
suggested the commercial traveller.   " I should
like to play this hand at Poker."

The millionaire glanced at his cards again and
remarked pleasantly, " Well, I don't care if I
do ; but you must let me discard and take this
queen."

" Oh, certainly," replied the commercial traveller eagerly ; " I'll bet you fifty dollars on my
hand."

" I will see that and go a hundred better," returned the miner.

The commercial traveller smiled with great glee ;
" I'll raise you two hundred and fifty," he said,
counting out four hundred dollars.

" Well," remarked the millionaire calmly, " if
you want to play Poker I'm your man.   I'll just
go you a thousand better."

This bold bet somewhat staggered the young

man, but he had confidence and a thousand dollars ; and he called.

"What have you?" asked the mine owner.

"I have four kings," the young man answered, throwing them on the board.

"Then I'll take the money," the millionaire remarked. "I have Four Aces," and he threw them down before the astonished commercial traveller.

"That's all right," said the latter, as soon as he had caught his breath. "That's all right — the money is yours ; but I'd like to know why in blazes did you take that queen?"

Thus we see that there can be finesse in Poker even as in Whist.

When the negro, black as the ace of spades, went to the late Canon Brookfield for a little temporary assistance, he began by saying: "I will not attempt to disguise from you, sir, that I am a man of color." And I will not attempt to disguise from you that the mining millionaire and the commercial traveller were gambling. We may hope that the loss of his money served the commercial traveller as a wholesome corrective of the gambling spirit, which is as different as possible from the spirit of scientific inquiry and self-improvement wherein one ought to play Poker. It is to be confessed at once that Poker differs from Whist and

from Chess, its chief rivals as an intellectual recreation, in that it *must* be played for money.   Chess
is usually its own reward ; and Whist can be, and
indeed often is, interesting without the attraction
of added money.   But in Poker the stakes must
have a definite pecuniary value or the game sinks
into mere child's play.   We play Poker for chips,
and chips must have a specie basis; in Poker, as in
the larger game of life, an irredeemable currency is
an unmixed evil.

So long, however, as the chips have a money
value, it is of very little importance how small that
value may be.   The genuine student and lover of
Poker will play his game, just the same, whether
the chip represents the French centime or the
American double-eagle.   The limit of a single bet
may be high or low as the circumstances warrant ;
it should be always at least twenty times the
smallest chip, and this smallest chip should be the
unit of the play, by which I mean it should be accepted as the proper ante.   As it is the limit which
makes the play high or low, this should always be
agreed on first, and then the value of the smallest
chip may be determined.   Unless the limit is at
least twenty times the smallest chip, the finest
points of artistic play are not possible, as the bluff
is barred ; and the power to bluff is an essential

part of Poker. A bluff is like the President's veto
—a most valuable device, but to be used sparingly
and only for good cause. With a proper proportion between the limit and the single chip, and a
proper proportion between the money value of
the chip and the private means of the players,
Poker is as free from taint of gambling as any
game can be.

In one of his most thoughtful essays Mark
Twain has recorded the result of a judicial attempt
to discover whether Old Sledge was or was not a
game of chance. The case came before a wise
judge in the far West ; the counsel for the defence
produced a cloud of witnesses who swore that
Old Sledge was a game of skill ; the prosecu-
tion brought forth testimony as abundant that it
was a game of chance ; so modern modification of
the ordeal by battle was accepted as decisive of the
issue. A jury of twelve was impanelled ; six of
the jurors were old players who maintained that
Old Sledge was a game of skill, and six were foolish young men who declared vainly that it was a
game of chance. The jury was locked up ; the six
couples of jurymen played against each other—
Skill *vs*. Luck. In less than an hour one of the
partisans of chance sent out to borrow more money ;
and before long the jury had agreed on their ver-

dict and were unanimously of the opinion that Old Sledge was a game of skill. So Whist is a game of skill; and so is Poker a game of skill.

Poker, like Whist, or the horse, or the annual rainfall, or anything else, may be used by the gambler to gamble with ; but Poker in itself is not a gambling game — it is purely scientific diversion. The element of chance which the novice may think paramount is in reality most insignificant. "Probability is the rule of life," said Bishop Butler, but in Poker probability is less concerned than in life-assurance, for example : and there is really no comparison to be made between it and any other game of cards. The proportion of luck to skill in winning at Whist, for instance, is almost exactly reversed in Poker ; the cards are quite 75 *per centum* of the game at Whist, but in Poker they are not 25 *per centum*. The most skilful player at Whist has not 25 *per centum* advantage over the most unskilful, but at Poker he has nearer to 75 *per centum* advantage. And character tells almost as much in playing Poker as skill. At its highest, Poker approaches the experiment in pure science; it is study in comparative psychology. In Poker there are no partners, no trumps turned, no tricks taken, no score kept, no game to make, and the cards themselves are of far less importance and significance than the character and temperament of the players. "The proper study of mankind is man," and Pope's essay would have been richer in observation and deeper in its truth had he had Poker to watch instead of the now obsolete Ombre. Poker is a true touchstone of character. In great trials a man generally tries to act as he ought, while in little affairs he shows himself as he really is. I know a gentleman who says he will allow no man to marry his daughter until he has tested his temper and gained an insight into his character by playing Poker with him.

And this is the game which Mr. Richard A. Proctor denounces with a vehemence akin to vituperation. "The existence and still more the flourishing condition of such a game as Poker, outside mere gambling dens, is one of the most portentous phenomena of American civilization," Mr. Proctor declares, because "the art which chiefly avails to help the gambler in playing this game is nothing more nor less than that art of which the enemy of man is proverbially said to be the father." The wise wit has told us that "sin has many tools, but a lie is a handle which fits them all," and Mr. Proctor refuses to take up a game which needs this handle. Mr. Proctor appears to be lacking in specific levity, as an Ameri-

can humorist called it. I fear me greatly that, had
he lived in the days of Swift, he would have insisted on an affidavit from Captain Lemuel Gulliver
before accepting that worthy navigator's account
of his voyages. I doubt, too, whether Mr. Proctor
would have had much patience with one Charles
Lamb, who was the author of biographies of Liston
and of Munden, in which there is no word of truth,
and who prided himself on being a matter-of-lie
man. Mr. Proctor seems to be impervious to humor; he takes life too seriously, and he judges
Poker too hastily.

In Poker there need be no lying and no deceit.
The essence of a lie is the intent to deceive.
Now in Poker there is no intent to deceive; there
is an effort to conceal, which is a very different
thing. Even the Bluff, which to Mr. Proctor is
inexpressibly wicked, is not an attempt to deceive; it is an attempt to drive the other player
off the field, not by deceiving him, but by so raising the stakes that he will not think the chance of
winning worth the price it would cost. If it were
not for the lying—which exists only in Mr. Proctor's misapprehension of the game—he thinks
Poker is not so bad after all. He comes to ban and
he stays to bless. In the first place, "the prob-
lems connected with the decision whether to stay

in or retire on a given hand are very pretty," so
he confesses ; and he finds later that one characteristic of the game " modifies the chances in a
very interesting manner," and that another characteristic " makes it a really excellent game for non-
gamblers, because calling so largely on the exer-
cise of judgment and also depending so much on
individual character" ; in fact, if the Bluff were
ruled out, and if the chips had no pecuniary value,
it would be one of the best and most amusing of
games. But, as I have tried to show, Mr. Proctor's objection to the Bluff is founded on a misun-
derstanding of its nature ; and his objection to
playing for money, so I learn from his later ' Whist
Chat,' does not extend to Whist, where "the
chief reason why money is staked is that the game
may be well and truly played." This is not
merely the chief reason why we play Poker with
chips representing money, but it is the only reason.

In the purely mathematical discussion of Poker
Principles and Chance Laws I sit at Mr. Proctor's
feet ; it is not for me to protest, even though I
think he has dealt harshly with the learned author
of the ' Complete Poker Player,' a treatise not
without faults and yet to be cherished and held in
high honor by all lovers of the scientific game ;
yet I cannot resist the temptation to suggest that

Mr. Proctor ought not to have been quite so hard
on the 'Complete Poker Player' for inadvertently
saying that a player drawing two cards to three
of a kind may get a Pair of a " denomination different from the Triplet," when he himself, with
like inadvertence, informs us that a " Full of three
aces and two threes beats a Full of three aces and
two deuces." No doubt the assertion is true, but
we should not like to see Mr. Proctor playing
Poker with a pack containing six aces. Nay,
more, if I may express the wish at the very bottom of my heart, I should prefer not to see Mr.
Proctor playing Poker at all. His mathematics are
all right, but he has no grip on the vital principles
of the game, and I am afraid an expert would find
him deficient both in theory and in practice. In
his later paper he intimates that certain frank
Americans told him that if he ever attempted
the game he would be " everlastingly beaten." I
know that when his earlier essay appeared there
was, on the part of every Poker player I met, a
wild longing to face Mr. Proctor across the green
cloth. I did what I could to allay this intense
desire, for I knew that such a feeling was not
scientific. But I must avow my belief that if Mr.
Proctor had ventured to play Poker his final condition would have been like that of the delinquent

in a certain case which came before a justice of the peace in a remote South-western State. The accused had been taken red-handed in the very act of Poker playing. To him the justice said sternly, "You were gambling?" The prisoner smiled feebly and answered, "No, jedge, no — not gambling." "But," returned the magistrate, "you were playing for money?" The prisoner replied meekly, "No, jedge, no — for chips." "Exactly," the justice continued, "and at the end of the game you cashed your chips and got your money?" The prisoner answered humbly, "No, jedge, no — at the end of the game I didn't have any chips!"

Mr. Proctor is much exercised in his mind as to the possibility of cheating at Poker, and apparently he thinks that it is frequent. Just how much false play there may be at Poker no one can declare precisely. All that one can say with certainty is that Poker does not give any greater privileges to the blackleg than any other game of cards. Robert-Houdin has shown us how easily the card-sharper may rob his victim at Écarté and Piquet. Even at Mr. Proctor's beloved Whist cheating is neither difficult nor infrequent. The advantage which an unscrupulous player may take over a confiding friend varies from a slight indelicacy to the gross-

est fraud. Mr. Hayward records an anecdote of
an English gentleman playing Whist with Count
Rechberg, formerly Secretary of Foreign Affairs in
Austria, and making so desperate, though successful, a finesse that His Excellency uttered an ex-
clamation of surprise, whereupon the gentleman
offered a bet that the Count himself should acknowledge that he had a sound reason for his play;
it was taken and then he coolly said, "Why, I
looked over your hand."   There are many degrees
between a peccadillo like this and the frank card-
sharping of Lord de Ros, whose exposure was "a
temporary discredit to Whist players," Mr. Hayward tells us, "for some of them were unluckily
seduced into acting on the penultimate Lord Hert-
ford's maxim : 'What would you do if you saw a
man cheating at cards?' 'Bet on him, to be sure.'"
And Barry Lyndon advises us to back a cheat,
of course.

These examples serve to show that there may
be serpents even in those earthly paradises, the
most select London clubs.   Mr. Jack Hamlin is a
far more dangerous opponent than Grog Davis.
Aubrey tells us that Sir John Suckling "played at
cards rarely well, and used to practice by himself
abed, and there studied the best way of managing
the cards."   Perhaps Sir John was guilty of a de-

vice now in fashion in Paris — so we learn from a recent readable account of 'Paris qui joue et Paris qui triche.' Play is very late at the Parisian clubs, and some players have a habit of going to bed in the afternoon so that they may come fresh to the card-table at night; a man who does this is said to *jouer le cadavre* — play the corpse. From this same work we learn that another American invention, "ringing in a cold deck," has long been known to French card-sharpers, who are adepts in *posant une portée.* I incline to the belief that Poker gives the cheat perhaps fewer chances than either Whist or Écarté; there are generally more players, for one thing, and, for another, there is less to distract their attention from the dealer. But the opportunities for trickery are abundant enough in any game. We had best beware of any player whose luck is unduly persistent; in course of time the Athenians tired of hearing Aristides always called the Just. However agreeable or liberal he may be, refrain from playing with him; fear the Greek even bearing gifts. The proper attitude toward the suspected player is that of the German-American in the familiar tale: he finds that he has four aces in his hand and his first impulse is to bet heavily; then he has a touch of caution and he asks, "Who dole dem carts?" "Jakey Einstein," is the answer. "Jakey Einstein?" he repeats, laying down his hand. "Den I pass out."

At all times we should insist, as did Mrs. Battle, on the rigor of the game, for nothing so conduces to cheating as the slovenly play which makes opportunity and temptation. The granting of license leads straight and quickly to the taking of liberties. The laws should be enforced without fear or favor. It is not formally prescribed in the code of the game that the blank card, sent out with every pack, shall be placed at the bottom after the cut; but the custom obtains in the playing of baccarat in the best French clubs, and it is advocated by the author of the ' Complete Poker Player.' If it were adopted at Poker and at Whist, dealing from the bottom of the pack would become difficult, if not impossible; Lord de Ros would have found his occupation gone; and the Rev. Thankful Smith, of the Thompson Street Poker Club, when he "was dealing, and knew by intuition that he would catch his fifth club," would not have been able to help himself quite as easily. Another point to be insisted upon is the showing of all the hands after a call. All the hands belong to the table, after a call, and must be shown. It is not sufficient that a player admits his defeat and throws away his hand. A card-sharper will sometimes confess that he is beaten if he has been called before much is bet, because he does not care to win too often and he prefers to show his hand only when there is enough profit to make it worth while. The laws of Poker, as given by Mr. Jones in the 'Encyclopædia Britannica,' do not cover this case.

The man who trumps his partner's ace at Whist will surely come to a bad end; and "the only excuse for not returning a trump is a fit of apoplexy or not having any." The man who plays Poker with the joker in, and who revels in jack-pots and who likes to start bucks, is a being quite as lost to all sense of shame as the man who trumps his partner's ace or refuses to return his partner's trump. In the strict rigor of the game (to which we should cling until we are in *rigor mortis*), there is no recognition of the intrusive joker, of the inexorable jack-pot, or of the itinerant buck, just as there is no recognition of Blazes, or of Skips, or of round-the-corner straights, or of the "Irish Flush"—five cards of one color but not of one suit, the acceptance of which has been suggested by the learned Dr. Pole. It cannot be said too often or too emphatically that the game of Poker is not like the pursuit of folk-lore, in which every variant is valuable and suggestive. Like the game of Whist, the game of Poker is now perfect and complete.   No man may now venture to improve on it, under penalty of spoiling its exquisite symmetry and simplicity.

Jack-pots are most intolerable and not to be endured, because they are wholly contrary to the true spirit of Poker.   The principle of Poker is the offering of an option at any moment.   At every change in the game a player has three courses open before him — he may raise, he may call, he may pass out.   For this free-will, the jack-pot substitutes predestination ; the theory of the jack-pot is that all the players *must* come in again and again until the pot is opened.   If a player is forced into the bastile of a jack-pot, his liberty is restrained, and he cannot play the true game of Poker.   And when the jack-pot is opened, there is little or no opportunity for the fine points of play ; the victory is always to the heavy battalions.   So we see that the jack-pot is an illogical excrescence on Poker ; it is a concession to the gambling spirit and a substitution of the brute force of mere chance for the delicate ingenuities of skill.   In its place the game of Jack-pots may be a good enough game for those who like it ; but it is not Poker, and it has nothing to do with Poker. The author of the ' Complete Poker Player ' notes that jack-pots are not popular in the South ; and I agree with him in his comment that "this last fact contains much promise, because the South is the conservative portion of the country, and may be relied on as the last resort of good sense in social matters."

The buck is an illegal monstrosity, to be abhorred of all good men. It is twin to the jackpot. It is to be avoided for the same reasons, because it is coercive and because it is gambling— and in the genuine game of Poker, liberty and skill go hand in hand. No man who takes pleasure in the sorry pastime known as "driving the bucks home" is capable of understanding the beauties of Poker. Far worse than he, however, is the man who plays Poker with the joker in. A man who does that will do anything. To the thoughtful mind no further argument is needed, beyond this use of the joker, to prove the existence of a personal devil and the doctrine of the total depravity of man. Only a totally depraved man, being prompted of the devil, could have invented the joker. There is in Poker, as I have shown, a fit and proper use for the blank card : it should be placed under the pack after the cut and before the deal.

The Joker and the Buck, Blazes and Skips, are

all signs of impure play, and these are often all to be found in a bastard game, which one may call Kindergarten-Poker and which bears the same relation to true Poker that Bumblepuppy does to Whist. In Kindergarten-Poker all the rules are relaxed and all possible varieties and vagaries of the game are cultivated. Most of the players never know who dealt nor who holds the age. They forget when it is their turn to come in and how much it costs. They never remember how many cards any one drew, and they are inclined to be indignant when their request for information on this point is denied after several bets have been made. They are always in doubt as to whether or not a Flush beats a Straight. They are prone to give aid and information to the enemy by throwing down their cards before it is their turn to do so ; for this crime no punishment can be too severe, and when a player has been convicted of it and pardoned and sins again impenitently, *la mort sans phrases* should be his swift fate.

Kindergarten-Poker, candor compels me to confess, is a great favorite with the ladies ; its license pleases their libertine souls, and its semblance to the true game lets them flatter themselves into the belief that they are actually playing Poker. Mr. Hayward applies to whist players the anecdote of

"the Italian who had the honor of teaching George
III. the violin," and who, on being asked by his
royal pupil what progress he was making, observed: "Please your Majesty, there are three
classes of players: 1, Those who cannot play at
all; 2, Those who play badly; 3, Those who
play well. Your Majesty is just rising into the
second class." This is the outside compliment
that we ought to pay to the most of the ladies
who fancy they play Poker. Woman is inclined
to be careless—and in Poker carelessness, even
in very little things, is highly dangerous. Woman
is inclined to be curious—and in Poker curiosity
is fatal. And yet woman does not fail wholly as
a Poker player, and this is because her unreason-
ing judgment, her feminine intuitions, her illogical
insight—to attempt to define roughly one of the
most precious and delicate of woman's gifts—often
enable her to snatch victory in the very moment
of defeat and disaster.

Of the more obvious types of Poker players
three demand and deserve consideration. These
are the Chatterer, the Silent Man, and the Coroner.
The Chatterer is the player who is persistent in
talking, who is given to the spinning of yarns,
whose tongue runs on and rattles along in the
presence of death or of Four Aces. But the Chat-

10

terer is not always a bad player—there is often
method in his madness; and now and again he is
not swept away by the flood of his own words.
There may be a keen eye and a quick brain above
the rapid tongue, and not unfrequently the Chatterer has prescience of the best time for passing
out. The Silent Man rarely opens his mouth save
to put a cigar into it; he lets his money talk for
him; he is always ready with his chips; he rarely
bluffs and he never shows his hand unnecessarily
or reveals a card in it. More frequently than not
he is a winner. He often takes a plain soda or a
glass of sherry when others accept the fragrant
julep or the seductive cocktail. When conversation becomes general and the game flags, while
the Chatterer is coming to the point of a good
story, he is wont to rap on the table impatiently
and to ask, "Oh, let's play Poker. What are we
here for, anyhow?" Then everybody comes in
sedately and sorrowfully, and he raises the ante
and they see the raise and he stands pat with a
Full. The Coroner is the player who insists on
holding a *post mortem* inquest on every departed
hand. We are told that talking it over, as the
ladies call it, fighting one's battles o'er, is one of
the best ways of learning Whist; but in Poker
the habit of holding an inquest on dead-and-gone

play is insufferable. The Coroner is also given to congratulating himself on hypothetical victories in supposititious draws. If ifs and ands were pots and pans, he'd always have the best of hands. When he is the dealer, the Coroner is prone to look at the cards he might have drawn had he come in; thus he gives himself the joy of winning many Barmecede pots.

General Schenck held that " the main elements of success in the game are good luck, good cards, plenty of cheek, and good temper." Of these good luck is by far the most important. Good luck is the prime requisite of the good player. Now good luck cannot be acquired by taking thought; it is congenital. The lucky man is born so, for no one ever achieved luck or had luck thrust upon him. Some men pass through life wreathed with four-leaved clovers and loaded down with horse-shoes, while others are born on Friday, the 13th of May, and have opals given to them in the cradle. As in the great game of Life, so at Poker. And by luck I mean no vain superstition. To the Poker player as to other wise men, luck is the name of an intangible total of innumerable influences; chief among these influences are the player's state of mind, and especially the state of his self-confidence. These, of

course, are conditions which vary from day to day.
There are others, as inscrutable and as inexorable,
inherent in every man's nature. I have heard it
asserted that the great family of the Rothschilds
never employs an unlucky man. It is not that
they are superstitious; it is that they are keen
enough to see behind the vulgar superstition a
solid scientific fact—the fact that there is always a
real cause for a man's bad luck, though this cause
cannot always be ascertained. In the unlucky
man there is wanting the something which makes
for success. This something may be a suitable defect of temper or of temperament, of character or
of training; it may be but a little thing in itself,
but it suffices; the man who has it is unlucky and
he does not succeed; *vae victis!*

Good luck the good Poker player must have, and
good cards;—and these things are not identical, for
one may have good cards often and lose only the
more, if just then the adversary happens to have
better. Good temper he should have also, and
plenty of cheek—though I do not like this term;
a resolute self-confidence and a willingness to take
the chances when once they have been calculated,
would serve to indicate better the fourth quality.
The great Poker player is born, like the poet, but
he is also made, like the orator. He must have

the dash and the light-heartedness of the French zouave; he must have the sound knowledge of life which distinguished the spectacled professors in the German *landwehr;* he must have the dogged resistance of the thin red line of the British infantry; and he must have the ingenuity and tenacity of the veterans of the Army of the Potomac. Mr. Hayward applies to the great Whist player "the famous passage which Lord Beaconsfield borrowed of M. Thiers describing the qualifications and responsibilities of a great commander," and we may apply it even more aptly to the great Poker player: "At the same moment he must think of the eve and the morrow—of his flanks and his reserve; he must calculate at the same time the state of the weather and the moral qualities of his men. . . . Not only must he think—he must think with the rapidity of lightning; for on a moment, more or less, depends the glory or the shame. Doubtless all this may be done in an ordinary manner by an ordinary man; as we see every day of our lives ordinary men making successful ministers of state, successful speakers, successful authors. But to do all this with genius is sublime."

Poe declared that "the best Chess player in Christendom may be little more than the best player of Chess; but proficiency in Whist implies capacity for success in all those more important undertakings in which mind struggles with mind." Poe set Whist above Chess because it had more of the very qualities in the possession of which Poker surpasses Whist ; I might say, perhaps more exactly, which the ideal Poker player needs more than the Whist player and has more occasion to use. The good player, according to Poe, " examines the countenance of his partner, comparing it skilfully with that of each of his opponents ; he considers the mode of assorting the cards in each hand ; often counting trump by trump and honor by honor through the glances bestowed by their holders upon each. He notes every variation of face as the play progresses, gathering a fund of thought from the differences in the expression of certainty, of surprise, of triumph, or chagrin. . . . He recognizes what is played through feint, by the air with which it is thrown upon the table. A casual or inadvertent word, the accidental dropping or turning of a card, with the accompanying anxiety or carelessness in regard to its concealment ; the counting of the tricks, with the order of their arrangement, embarrassment, hesitation, eagerness, or trepidation—all afford, to his apparently intuitive perception, indications of the true state of affairs."

With obvious changes, this description applies more exactly to the Poker player than to the Whist player, for the observations which are of secondary importance in Whist are a prime necessity in Poker.

The great Poker players of the world have been very few; nature is not lavish with her treasures. I have heard that Daniel Webster (that steam-engine in trousers, as the Rev. Sydney Smith called him), who was a great lawyer and a great statesman, was also a great Poker player. Before the perfected pianoforte there could have been no great pianist; and we might as well look for a great pianist trained on the early clavecin, as expect to find a great Poker player before Gleek and Post-and-pair and Brag had developed into the perfect Poker. Else had I suggested that Shakspere would have been the greatest of Poker players. His large views of life, his keen insight into the mysterious play of motive, and his unexampled knowledge of his fellow-man would have furnished forth a splendid equipment for success as a Poker player. It has been proved to the satisfaction of those offering the evidence that Shakspere was a lawyer, a doctor, a traveller, a Jesuit and, in fact, many other things which he was not. But no one has yet suggested that he spent the years of his life, which are unaccounted for, as a man well might who had to live by his wits, in gaming, whereby he earned his living. The playing of Gleek, if indeed it be a ruder and more rudimentary Poker, would have been a fine school for the study of man. This suggestion explains many allusions in the sonnets ; yet it is but a supposition, no better than others which have been seriously urged, and, of a certainty, no worse. It is open to us to believe that the wit combats at the Mermaid between Shakspere and Ben Jonson were perhaps a measuring of wits across the card-table, and that, on the smaller space as on the larger, Jonson vied and revied in vain with Shakspere—Jonson "solid but slow in his performances," Shakspere, who, "lighter in sailing, could turn with all tides, tack about, and take advantage of all winds by the quickness of his wit and invention."

But if Shakspere never had the privilege of playing Poker himself, he has left us the portrait of one who, had he not lived before there were either playing-cards or Poker, would have been the greatest of Poker players—the Mark Antony of 'Julius Cæsar.' Cassius calls Antony "a masker and a reveller," but he fears "we shall find him a shrewd contriver." Brutus confesses, "I do lack some part of that quick spirit that is in Antony,"

and declares that " he is given to sports, to wild-
ness, and much company." Cæsar, referring to
Cassius, complains that " he loves no plays as thou
dost, Antony,"—and perhaps " he loves not play "
is a new reading not unworthy of consideration.
Antony is magnanimous ; he sees the nobility of
Brutus ; he has a true insight into the characters
of Lepidus and Octavius : each is treated differently and with equal tact. Antony is both bold
and wily, cunning and courageous. He has
promptness of decision and a swift certainty of
action. Above all, he believes in himself, the first
step toward making others believe in him. Consider the marvellous skill of the speech in the
forum over Cæsar's body—surely the best bit of
Poker-talk in the history of the world. To have
seen Mark Antony,—Shakspere's Mark Antony,
not the mere Mark Antony of history,—to have
seen him playing Poker would be an inexpressible
joy to all those who have felt the fascination of the
game. I can hardly imagine a pleasanter Shaks-
perean fantasy than the authorized report of a
game of Poker between half a dozen of Shakspere's men—Mark Antony for one, and jolly Sir
John Falstaff for another ; the merry Mercutio for
a third ; for a fourth the humorous Jacques, who
should suck melancholy from the game as from an

egg ; for a fifth Sir Toby Belch, though perhaps the knight is over given to cakes and ale, whereas your true Poker player is sober and gets his sensual pleasure out of the game itself; while the gallant Benedick should be the sixth, with the sharp-tongued and large-hearted Beatrice looking over his shoulder.

AN EPISTLE

To Master Brander Matthews, writer, on the occasion of his putting forth a book entitled "Pen and Ink."

—

New London, Conn., Sept. 10, 1888.

Dear Brander:

        I have known thee long, and found
Thee wise in council, and of judgment sound;
Steadfast in friendship, sound and clear in wit,
And more in virtues than may here be writ.
But most I joy, in these machine-made days,
To see thee constant in a craftsman's ways;
That the plain tool that knew thy 'prentice hand
Gathers no rust upon thy writing-stand;
That no Invention saves the labor due
To any Task that's worth the going through;
That now when butter snubs the stranger churn,
Plain pen and ink still serve a writer's turn.
Though I, more firmly orthodox, still hold,
In dire default of quills, to steel or gold,
And though thy pen be rubber — let it pass —
A breath of blemish on thy soul's clear glass.

There is no "writing fluid" in thy pot,
But honest ink of nutgall brew, God wot!
Thou dost not an electric needle ply
And, like a housewife with an apple-pie,
Prick thy fair page into a stencil-plate —
Then daub with lampblack for a duplicate.
Nor thine the sloven page whereon the shirk
With the rough tool attempts the finished work,
And introduces to the sight of men
The Valet Pencil for the Master Pen.

Not all like thee! in this uneasy age,
When more by trick than toil we earn our wage.
Here by the sea a gentle poet dwells,
And in fair leisure weaves his magic spells;
And yet doth dare with countenance serene
To weave them on a tinkling steel machine,
Where an impertinent and soulless bell
Rings, at each finished line, a jangling knell.
The muse and I, we love him, and I think
She MAY forgive his slight to pen and ink,
And let no dull mechanic cam or cog
The lightsome movement of his metres clog;
But oh! I grieve to see his fingers toy
With this base slave in dalliance close and coy,
While in his standish dries the atrid spring
Where hides the shyer muse that loves to sing.

Give me the old-time ink, black, flowing, free,
And give, oh, give! the old goose-quill to me—
The goose-quill, whispering of humility.

It whispers to the bard: "Fly not too high!
You *flap your wings*—remember, so could I.
I cackled in my lifetime, it is true;
But yet again remember, so do You.
And there were some things possible to me
That possible to you will never be.
I stood for hours on one columnar leg,
And, if my sex were such, could lay an egg.
Oh, well for you, if you could thus beget
Material for your morning omelette;
Or, if things came to such a desperate pass,
You could in calm contentment nibble grass!
Conceited bard! and can you sink to rest
Upon the feather-pillow of your breast?"

Hold, my dear Brander, to your pot of ink:
The muse sits poised upon that fountain's brink.
And that you long may live to hold a pen
I'll breathe a prayer;
                The world will say "Amen!"

H. C. BUNNER.

Demco, Inc. 38-293